Letting Go of
PERFECT

SECOND EDITION

Letting Go of
PERFECT

Empower Children to Overcome Perfectionism

Jill L. Adelson, Ph.D.,
and Hope E. Wilson, Ph.D.

PRUFROCK PRESS INC.
WACO, TEXAS

Library of Congress Control Number: 2021935071

Copyright ©2021, Prufrock Press Inc.

Edited by Stephanie McCauley

Cover and layout design by Allegra Denbo
Illustrations by David Parker

ISBN-13: 978-1-64632-101-8

Printed in the United States of America.

At the time of this book's publication, all facts and figures cited are the most current available. All telephone numbers, addresses, and website URLs are accurate and active. All publications, organizations, websites, and other resources exist as described in the book, and all have been verified. The author and Prufrock Press Inc. make no warranty or guarantee concerning the information and materials given out by organizations or content found at websites, and we are not responsible for any changes that occur after this book's publication. If you find an error, please contact Prufrock Press Inc.

Prufrock Press Inc.
P.O. Box 8813
Waco, TX 76714-8813
Phone: (800) 998-2208
Fax: (800) 240-0333
https://www.prufrock.com

Dedication

This book is dedicated to my husband, Jonathan, and to my children, Caleb, Zoe, and Emma. Their patience, support, and belief in me has helped me grow and accomplish as a researcher, mother, and person. It also is dedicated to my former students at B. C. Charles who taught me at least as much as I taught them.—*Jill*

This book is dedicated to my children, Lily and Keenan, and my parents, Ted and Chris, who have endlessly supported me throughout this journey. Thank you to all of my network of family and friends who come together when life gets tough. I would also like to dedicate this book to all of my students, past and present, who will go on to inspire a generation of students to come.—*Hope*

Table of Contents

Acknowledgments   ix

A Note to the Reader   xi

CHAPTER 1   Perfectionism and Children   1

CHAPTER 2   Debunking Myths About Perfectionism   7

CHAPTER 3   The Academic Achiever
"Must Achieve 100%"   25

CHAPTER 4   The Aggravated Accuracy Assessor
"Exactness and Fixation on 'Redos'"   37

CHAPTER 5   The Risk Evader
"All or Nothing"   55

CHAPTER 6   The Controlling Image Manager
"I Could Have if I Wanted to"   65

CHAPTER 7   The Procrastinating Perfectionist
"If It Stays in My Mind, Then I Can't Fail"   75

CHAPTER 8   Identifying Healthy Motivation and Goals
and Unhealthy Perfectionism   89

CHAPTER 9   Strategies for the Classroom   97

CHAPTER 10   Strategies for the Home   123

CHAPTER 11   Resources for Children   137

CHAPTER 12   Resources for Adults   147

Glossary   155

References   165

About the Authors   177

Acknowledgments

IN the first edition of this book, we acknowledged and thanked those who inspired us to study perfectionism, our first Prufrock Press editor, and an educator who tried some of our suggestions with her students. We have grown as scholars, educators, parents, and writers in the 12 years between editions.

Here we would like to acknowledge those who have helped us grow in the last 12 years. Jill would like to acknowledge and thank the strong women in academia and research who have supported and mentored her along the way, including but in no way limited to Hope, Kate Snyder, Lisa Keller, Ann Robinson, Catherine Little, Betsy McCoach, and Rena Subotnik. Hope would like to acknowledge the brilliant colleagues who have been role models in navigating the world of academia, family, and research, including (just a few of the many) Diane Yendol-Hoppy, Kally Malcom, Erin Morris-Miller, Anne Rinn, and, of course, Jill.

We also would like to thank Olivia Santos for her work in gathering the research articles that were published between the writing of the first and second edition of this book.

A Note to the Reader

FAMILY and educator communication is critical for the health and wellness of our children. Oftentimes, children's behavior does not present itself the same way in the home and in the classroom, and both families and educators should know the behaviors and tendencies that occur in each setting. Moreover, by working as a team, families and educators can better determine which strategies are working and which ones are not. We considered focusing this book for only one audience, either families or educators. However, we believe that both parts of this team should be aware of how behaviors may be manifested in each environment and what strategies may be useful in each setting so that the work families and educators do can be complementary and not redundant; this approach also helps facilitate communication between families and educators about strategies to employ. We believe that families and educators are both working toward the same goal, and thus a book directed to both audiences can help develop understandings.

In this book, you will find scenarios presented in the Chapters 3–7 about the types of perfectionistic tendencies. These were scenarios that we witnessed in the classroom and are based on real children and their behaviors (with their names changed). We have reviewed and added to the strategies since the first edition, but many of the stories and strategies have remained unchanged. The biggest change between the two editions is that this edition reflects the latest in research on perfectionism. In particular, Chapters 1, 2, and 8 have been updated and revised to reflect what researchers have learned about perfectionism in the last 12 years as well as the our more mature, nuanced understanding of perfectionism. We also have updated the resources list, adding additional books, games, and websites, including sections on mindfulness and for families in crisis.

We also would like to acknowledge that we attempted to make this new edition more inclusive. Rather than "he or she," we now refer to "they." In most cases, we refer to "families" or "caregivers" instead of "parents," and "educators" instead of "teachers" as well.

CHAPTER 1

Perfectionism and Children

Chances are that you are reading this book because you are concerned about a child, either your own or one in your class, who has exhibited perfectionistic behaviors. It may be that you are concerned about your child's stress levels, the lack of joy your child takes in the process of creating, or the overly developed **self-criticism** they demonstrate. Perhaps your child has an obsession with mistakes and "flaws," sheds tears over small errors and perceived imperfections, or tends toward **procrastination** and **fear of failure**. When perfectionism becomes unhealthy and begins to affect everyday life, we, as adults, become concerned for our children and want to help them, but we often are at a loss for what to do.

> Note that **words in bold** are defined in the glossary in the back of the book!

In the roles of parent and teacher, we have struggled with how to help children use their **motivation** and high goals in a healthy way instead of becoming paralyzed, frustrated, anxious, and stressed by perfectionistic tendencies. This book stemmed from a case study observing Jill's fourth graders and noting their perfectionistic behaviors (Adelson, 2007). From this case study, she identified five types of perfectionism. Between the two of us, we have worked with hundreds of children, including our own children, and have had the opportunity to use the strategies we suggest. Of course, there is no one solution to helping your child overcome perfectionism. Hopefully, this book will give you some ideas that will help you work with your child and create an environment that encourages risk-taking, acknowledges mistakes as learning experiences, supports short-term as well as long-term **goal setting**, and celebrates accomplishments, the process, and personal areas of strength. As a parent (or other caregiver) and/ or educator, you can serve as a role model, support system, and a source of guidance to a child who exhibits perfectionistic tendencies. With your help, your child can let go of unhealthy perfectionism. However, it will not happen overnight. This process takes time. As Corinne, one of Jill's fourth-grade students, said, "Really, the only way to overcome perfectionism is to accept it and consistently tell yourself it doesn't have to be perfect. Over time, with the maturity of growing up and the consistency of your corrections, it will level out." To help the children we love, we must help them both to understand their perfectionistic tendencies and to learn to use their motivation and high goals in healthy ways.

If your child displays clinical symptoms, such as talking about **suicide**, a depressed mood, general anxiety, or loss of appetite, be sure to seek professional help. In fact, the symptoms of **depression**, **anxiety disorders**, and even things like **Attention Deficit/Hyperactivity Disorder (ADHD)** or **processing disorders** (which can contribute to perfectionism) are easily missed, even by the most diligent caregiver, so do not hesitate to seek help from a school counselor, community advocate, psychologist, or therapist.

> "Really, the only way to overcome perfectionism is to accept it and consistently tell yourself it doesn't have to be perfect. . . ." —Corinne, Newport News, VA

The strategies in this book are meant as a guide for families and educators to help children who are beginning to struggle with perfectionism. However, perfectionism at a young age can lead to more serious conditions, such as suicide, **eating disorders**, depression, and anxiety disorders as it progresses. Perfectionism also can be a symptom of underlying **psychological distress**. Many families, ours included, have found the help of licensed psychologists, therapists, and mental health counselors to be meaningful when extra support is needed. We provide resources in Chapters 11 and 12.

What Is Perfectionism?

Perfectionism generally refers to setting unreasonably high expectations of oneself, including an intolerance of mistakes. As you read this book, you will see that this can manifest itself in many ways. For example, in the classroom, it might look like a hyperfocus on grades, **procrastination**, or avoiding academic risks.

No one is a perfectionist in all parts of their life at all times. In fact, we know from the research that people (including kids) tend to be perfectionistic in specific areas (such as school, sports, or personal appearance) rather than in all areas of their life (e.g., Stoeber & Stoeber, 2009). Therefore, in this book we try to refer to **perfectionistic behaviors** or **perfectionistic tendencies** rather than to perfectionists, recognizing that perfectionism should not define a child's identity and likely is only a problem in one or two areas of life. Your decision to read this book suggests that you have recognized perfectionistic behaviors in a child you want to help.

Having strong **motivation** and high **goals** can be very positive. With motivation and high yet **realistic goals**, a person may focus on improvement through revision and practice, on goal setting and planning on how to reach those goals, and on developing their potential and abilities. However, perfectionistic behaviors and tendencies can cause stress, anxiety, fear, self-doubts, low **self-esteem**, and procrastination.

Perfectionism can be classified in several ways. One way to classify perfectionism is based on the perception of where the pressure to "be perfect" originates from, either internal or external (e.g., Flett et al., 2016; Gaudreau, 2012). **Self-oriented perfectionism** occurs when a child feels the internal drive for unreasonably high expectations. **Socially prescribed perfectionism** occurs when a child's desire for perfection is perceived to come from their social context (i.e., family, educators, coaches, friends, or even media). Some children are considered to be a mixed type, in that they feel pressure both internally and from social contexts.

Some researchers and practitioners also classify perfectionism by the ways in which children think about their actions. Some children (and adults) focus on mistakes and errors, which is sometimes called **evaluative concerns perfectionism** or self-criticism perfectionism and is generally considered to lead to unhealthy outcomes (Burgess et al., 2016). Other people focus on setting high personal expectations, called **personal standards perfectionism**. Many researchers, including us, consider being motivated and having high goals and expectations generally to be healthy, and consider perfectionism to come into play when those expectations become unrealistic and unhealthy. That **unrealistic goals** (often used as evidence for unhealthy perfectionism) may be conflated with general high personal expectations (that are healthy) may be one reason that research has not yet come to a clear conclusion about whether or not this type of perfectionism leads to unhealthy outcomes (Dunkley, Blankstein, & Berg, 2012). Additionally, people may have both high evaluative concerns and high personal standards (called **mixed-type perfectionism**) or neither (called **nonperfectionism**; Damian et al., 2014). Research has shown differing results about the relative negative effects of nonperfectionism and mixed-type perfectionism on children (Damian et al., 2014).

The goals of this book are to help children overcome perfectionism, be able to set appropriate and meaningful goals, and continue to strive for high achievement without the barriers that the anxiety around perfectionism can cause. According to Hamachek (1978), children who can move to this state of mind "derive a real sense of pleasure from the labors of a painstaking effort," and they "feel free to be less precise as the situation permits" (p. 27). This is the goal we want for children exhibiting perfectionistic behaviors and tendencies. We hope the strategies suggested in this book will help you move children toward this type of orientation, allowing them to take pleasure in the process and recognize that they do not need to strive for absolute perfection at all times.

About This Book

The next chapter of this book provides you more background information about perfectionism. We provide you an overview of the research on perfectionism by debunking seven myths about perfectionism. This chapter will help you understand some common misconceptions about perfectionism and how these myths might apply to your child.

Chapters 3 through 7 introduce each of the five types of perfectionists: the **Academic Achiever**, the **Aggravated Accuracy Assessor**, the **Risk Evader**, the **Controlling Image Manager**, and the **Procrastinating Perfectionist** (Adelson, 2007). First, we present vignettes that describe children exhibiting behaviors characteristic of that type of perfectionist. These are based on the children we have worked with and observed. Then, we describe the characteristics of that type of perfectionist. Following the description, we provide strategies for the classroom and for the home to help students who exhibit this type of perfectionism use it in a healthy manner. We encourage educators and families to consider the strategies in both sections, as what truly helps children is when educators and families work together to support them. By considering both sections, you might find complementary ways to support your child.

After the five types of perfectionism, we help you identify traits of unhealthy perfectionism. Chapter 8 includes a list of behaviors characteristic of each of the five types of perfectionists, a list of signs of perfectionism, a description of healthier patterns of behavior, and a list of tools you can use to identify perfectionistic tendencies in children.

> *We encourage educators and families to consider the strategies both for the classroom and for the home because what truly helps children is when educators and families work together to support them.*

Having established what perfectionism is, identified the traits of unhealthy perfectionism, and examined the five types of perfectionism, we then provide what many educators and families are wanting—an overview of strategies to help children overcome perfectionism in the classroom (Chapter 9) and in the home (Chapter 10), leading them to have good motivation and set high but realistic goals. Each of these chapters begins with a table reviewing the strategies we recommend for each of the five types of perfectionism. Although we encourage you to read the individual chapters for more detailed descriptions, each table provides a summary of those strategies. In Chapter 9, we share general strategies for the classroom, which are followed by specific activities for the classroom. These include suggestions to be used within existing classroom activities, like **formative assessment**, as well as specific activities addressing perfectionism. In Chapter 10, we review the strategies for the five types of perfectionism with methods to be used in **crisis moments**. Next, we provided general strategies and discussion suggestions for you and your child as well as suggestions for family time. Chapter 10 ends by addressing a time during which many families struggle to help their child with perfectionism—homework time.

> *Our goal is not to eliminate having high goals and standards but to help children take pleasure in the process, appreciate their strengths, see their mistakes as learning experiences, and recognize that they should not expect perfection at all times.*

We hope you will find this book helpful for creating a positive environment and supporting your young child who is experiencing perfectionism. However, there are other resources to help you further. In Chapter 11, we provide some suggested resources for children, including picture and chapter books and games. Then, in Chapter 12, we provide resources for adults, including books, articles, websites, and hotlines.

At the end of this book you will find a glossary and a list of references. We have provided definitions for each of the bold words in the book. The references are a good resource if you want to read more about research on perfectionism, especially in **academically gifted children**.

CHAPTER 2

Debunking Myths About Perfectionism

Myths about perfectionism are perpetuated through social media, blogs, and popular media. This chapter outlines seven of the most common beliefs about perfectionism and what researchers have found to support or to debunk them. Experts in the field have used **scientific techniques** and **observational techniques** to learn about perfectionism among both adults and children. To give you an understanding of this research, we will share how it applies to commonly held beliefs about perfectionism. Finally, we add some practical applications of the research for your life with children who exhibit perfectionistic tendencies and behaviors. Table 1 summarizes the seven myths about perfectionism.

TABLE 1
The Seven Myths About Perfectionism

1. Perfectionism is primarily a problem for the intellectually gifted.
2. The causes of perfectionism are largely unknown.
3. There is only one type of perfectionist.
4. The identification of perfectionism is merely anecdotal.
5. Perfectionism is a fixed personality trait.
6. Adults cannot do anything to help young perfectionists.
7. Perfectionism is not really that harmful for children.

Myth 1: Perfectionism Is Primarily a Problem for the Intellectually Gifted

Many caregivers, educators, researchers, and authors have characterized perfectionism as a problem that only affects the gifted or high-achieving population (Callard-Szulgit, 2003). Perfectionism is a condition that often is addressed in textbooks and materials concerning the social and emotional development of gifted students. Educators tend to associate perfectionism primarily with students who they believe have high abilities or those in advanced classes. In fact, perfectionism has almost become a trademark characteristic of students who are in honors, Advanced Placement, or International Baccalaureate classes in secondary school.

> *Many studies have shown perfectionism among students of varying ability levels.*

What the Research Says

Research, on the other hand, does not support this opinion. Although many researchers and professionals in the field of gifted education conceptualize perfectionism as a problem primarily for gifted students, many studies have shown perfectionism among students of varying ability levels. When perfectionism scales are given to students of all ability levels, studies show that students identified as gifted are no more likely to exhibit perfectionistic tendencies than students not identified as gifted (Ogurlu, 2020). Remember the distinction that we and other researchers make— that those exhibiting perfectionism have *unrealistic* goals. Although many gifted children have high goals, especially because they can perform at a high level, that does not necessarily mean they have unrealistic goals that damage their self-esteem.

Other research indicates that students with varying levels of ability, from varying backgrounds, and in varying domains experience perfectionism (e.g., Flett et al., 1998; Frost & Marten, 1990; Stoeber & Stoeber, 2009; Suddarth & Slaney, 2001). Studies have found perfectionism among various groups of students, including athletes (Hill et al., 2012), racially and ethnically diverse students (Rice et al., 2008), and students with learning disabilities (O'Brien, 2005; Saddler & Buckland, 1995), as well as in cross-cultural studies of international populations (e.g., Maksic & Iwasaki, 2009). Similarly, perfectionism was found in samples of both above-average and average-ability mathematics students in the Czech Republic (Parker et al., 2001). Thus, it is apparent from research that perfectionism can affect children from many backgrounds and with diverse ability and achievement levels.

However, research also indicates that perfectionism is **domain-specific**, meaning that people exhibiting perfectionistic tendencies tend to focus this trait on particular areas of their lives (e.g., athletics, academics, personal appearance, or social engagement). Preliminary research seems to indicate that intellectually gifted students are more likely to have academic-specific perfectionism, as compared to college athletes, who (perhaps unsurprisingly) focus their perfectionism on their performance in sports (e.g., Stoeber & Stoeber, 2009). This may indicate that although perfectionism is present across the entire spectrum of the population, it is manifested in different ways for gifted children.

Summary of Myth 1

Perfectionism certainly is an issue that is associated closely with gifted students, but that does not necessarily indicate that the gifted population is more likely to exhibit perfectionistic tendencies than the general population. Children may direct perfectionistic behaviors and tendencies toward varying aspects of their lives, such as athletics, fine arts, or hobbies. **Academically gifted children** may be more likely to direct their perfectionism toward schoolwork, thus capturing the attention of educators and families. Educators and families of all children should be aware of the negative aspects of perfectionism and to provide opportunities for students to adapt their characteristics to a more positive approach. Giftedness is certainly not a prerequisite for perfectionism, and perfectionism may not exhibit itself in the area of schoolwork.

> *Giftedness is certainly not a prerequisite for perfectionism, and perfectionism may not exhibit itself in the area of schoolwork.*

Myth 2: The Causes of Perfectionism Are Largely Unknown

Educators and families tend to throw up their hands in confusion as to why some children seem to exhibit perfectionistic tendencies more than others. Certainly, perfectionism is a product of a person's personality, but what factors contribute to it? Although there is no formula that results in perfectionism, it truly is a result of both nurture and nature. Researchers have shown that some characteristics of a child's environment can contribute to the development of perfectionistic behaviors and tendencies.

What the Research Says

One habit of mind that research has linked to perfectionism is **dichotomous thinking** (He, 2016), or the tendency to view events in life as either bad or good, with little or no gray area in between. When tasks are seen as either complete successes or failures—and by association, one's sense of self becomes either a success or failure—perfectionism is a natural consequence (Egan et al., 2012). Any error or mistake, or not quite meeting an exceptionally high expectation, can lead a child with dichotomous thinking to believe that they are a complete failure. For example, a child may come to you in tears because they "failed" an exam, but when you look at their paper, they made an 89!

Another precursor to perfectionism may be what researchers call **rumination**, or a fixation on interactions and events in the past (Flett et al., 2011). This can look like excessive worry over mistakes made or social missteps. It is also characterized by an **internal dialogue** that cycles through these past events over and over again—sometimes to the point at which it interferes with daily life. People who ruminate tend to have more serious negative outcomes from their perfectionism (Harris et al., 2008), but studies are inconclusive on if the thoughts cause the perfectionistic tendencies or vice versa. It is likely that this relationship is reciprocal, in that each contributes to the severity of the other, intensifying the symptoms of both.

Parents play an important role in the development of perfectionistic behaviors and tendencies in young people. Some studies indicate that children with perfectionism often have parents who are also perfectionists (Cook & Kearney, 2009, 2014; Frost et al., 1991). **Parenting style** also factors into perfectionistic tendencies. Specifically, **authoritarian parenting** is more closely linked to perfectionism than **authoritative** or **permissive** types (Gong et al., 2015; Kenney-Benson & Pomerantz, 2005; Miller et al., 2012; Siegle & Schuler, 2000). Authoritarian parenting is characterized by strict and inflexible disciplinary styles with less nurturing and more criticism.

More specifically, inconsistent or nonexistent approval, combined with criticism from caregivers, can lead to perfectionism in children, as can parental approval that is conditional to a child's performance (Craddock et al., 2009). American parents of perfectionists tend to have high standards for their children and have a high need for organization (O'Leary & Schuler, 2003). On the other hand, a parent's ability to nurture children (DiPrima et al., 2011), as well as their focus on **learning goals** rather than **performance goals** (Ablard & Parker, 1997), makes a difference in a child developing healthier habits of mind, motivation, and goal orientation. Finally, family environments that are flexible (rather than rigidly structured) and include task-involving (rather than performance-oriented) activities nurture healthy attitudes toward achievement, rather than perfectionistic ones (McArdle & Duda, 2004). In this type of environment, caregivers are involved with their children in everyday tasks and family activities. Parenting style and family environment clearly effect the development of perfectionism in children.

> *Caregivers play an important role in the development of perfectionistic behaviors and tendencies in young people.*

Summary of Myth 2

Some factors contributing to perfectionism cannot be changed; however, other personality and environmental contributors can be altered to help a child overcome perfectionism and exhibit strong motivation with realistic goals. Families, educators, and counselors can work with children to change dichotomous thinking into a healthier mode of perception, recognizing that mistakes are acceptable and that a flaw does not make a person a failure. Parenting styles that focus on mistakes, performance goals, and harshness and that withhold acceptance contribute to perfectionism among children. Adapting a parenting style that focuses more on learning from mistakes and on positive accomplishments in all tasks may help children develop healthy ways of approaching goals and achievement.

Myth 3: There Is Only One Type of Perfectionist

Educators and families tend to categorize students as either perfectionists or nonperfectionists. In this conception, all perfectionists fit the same set of characteristics and are marked by similar behaviors, motivations, and outcomes. However, research suggests that perfectionism can be categorized by many different variables (e.g., Dixon et al., 2004), including the orientation and the ways in which perfectionistic thoughts manifest.

What the Research Says

Some researchers have identified three orientations of perfectionism: self-oriented, other-oriented, and socially prescribed perfectionism (Blankstein et al., 2007; Speirs Neumeister, 2004). **Self-oriented perfectionism** is characterized by a strong sense of self-criticism and internal need for high expectations. In this type of perfectionism, the child holds themselves to extremely high, unrealistic standards. **Socially prescribed perfectionism** occurs when a child believes that other people, or society at large, holds them to unrealistically high standards and are critical of their mistakes. These external influences may be from adults (e.g., caregivers, educators, or coaches), peer groups, media influences (e.g., social media, television, marketing), or a combination of these. Remember that these pressures are perceived by the child and may or may not actually be exerted on the child from the outside source. For example, a child may feel like a caregiver is putting pressure on them to make straight A's when the caregiver has no such expectation at all. Finally, **other-oriented perfectionism** is when a child holds other people to unrealistically high standards and perfection. This type of perfectionism, at the most extreme, is associated with antisocial behaviors, narcissism, and sociopathy (Dimaggio & Attinà, 2012). Table 2 describes characteristics of these three types of perfectionists.

Additionally, a person may exhibit a combination of these orientations. A child could feel pressure to meet high expectations from both external and internal sources, which is typically classified as a mixed orientation. Conversely, people who do not seem to hold unrealistically high expectations for themselves or for others are classified as nonperfectionists.

> *A child may feel like a caregiver is putting pressure on them to make straight A's when the caregiver has no such expectation at all.*

Another way perfectionism is classified is by the ways in which the perfectionistic thoughts manifest, called personal standards perfectionism or evaluative concerns perfectionism. Those with **personal standards perfectionism** focus on unrealistically high standards for performance, tending to look at the overall evaluation of the performance and if it meets the high expectations present (Burgess et al., 2016). On the other hand, those with **evaluative concerns perfectionism** focus on errors, mistakes, and missteps (Burgess et al., 2016). In general, evaluative concerns perfectionism is considered more maladaptive, leading to worse outcomes and greater self-criticism.

Researchers have also found that people may display a **mixed-type perfectionism**, in which a person holds both high personal standards and high evaluative concerns (Stoeber, 2012). The outcomes for this type are hotly debated in the research, with some studies finding that the personal standards act as resilience factor, helping to mediate the negative effects of the evaluative concerns (Inglés et al., 2016). Other studies, however, found that holding high personal standards and evaluative concerns magnify the

TABLE 2
Self-Oriented, Socially Prescribed, and Other-Oriented Perfectionism

Self-Oriented Perfectionism	Socially Prescribed Perfectionism	Other-Oriented Perfectionism
• Self-critical • Internally motivated • Has strong personal standards	• Susceptible to peer pressure • Motivated by others • Concerned with appearance to others	• Critical of others • May have difficulty maintaining relationships • Holds others to high standards
See "Academic Achiever"	See "Controlling Image Manager"	Less researched than other types of perfectionism

negative outcomes of perfectionism (Damian et al., 2014). See Table 3 for a summary of these three types.

Finally, it is possible to combine these two classification systems. For example, someone can have socially prescribed perfectionism that is primarily focused on evaluative concerns, meaning that they are overly concerned with how others perceive the mistakes that they make.

Summary of Myth 3

In addition to these models, we have observed distinct patterns of perfectionistic tendencies and behaviors in children that align in many ways to the research paradigms presented here. We have classified these behaviors into the following categories: the Academic Achiever, the Aggravated Accuracy Assessor, the Risk Evader, the Controlling Image Manager, and the Procrastinating Perfectionist. Table 4 describes each category briefly, delineating a few characteristics of each. These categories are not exclusive of one another, but much like the classifications in the research literature, they can overlap. These categories capture general perfectionistic behaviors observed in gifted classrooms. Each of these profiles will be discussed in further detail in the following chapters.

TABLE 3
Personal Standards, Evaluative Concerns, and Mixed-Type Perfectionism

Personal Standards Perfectionism	Evaluative Concerns Perfectionism	Mixed-Type Perfectionism
• Has high standards for performance • Has high expectations for performance can be unrealistic	• Focuses on errors and mistakes • Tends to be critical of self and prone to stress	• Combines both types • Many researchers think this type has worse outcomes than other types
See "Academic Achiever"	See "Aggravated Accuracy Assessor"	Note that a child may fall into more than one "type"

Myth 4: The Identification of Perfectionism Is Merely Anecdotal

Families and educators often wonder if there is a formal way to identify the children in their lives who might have perfectionism. Aside from the vast amount of anecdotal information that families and educators gather every day about a child's behavior, attitudes, and thought processes, adults would like a uniform way to measure perfectionism in children. Fortunately, researchers have developed a variety of measures of perfectionism, both to identify people who are in need of clinical interventions and to study perfectionism within populations of people.

What the Research Says

The **instruments** available to measure perfectionism reflect the theories held by the authors and developers of each test. The Multidimensional Perfectionism Scale (Parker & Stumpf, 1995; Sondergeld et al., 2007) and the Childhood Multidimensional Perfectionism Scale (DeKryger, 2005) measure the three orientations of perfectionism (self-oriented, socially prescribed, and other-oriented). The Almost Perfect Scale–Revised (Rice et al., 2007; Vandiver & Worrell, 2002), on the other hand, measures per-

TABLE 4
Profiles of Perfectionists

Academic Achievers	Hold unrealistically high expectations for their performance in academic pursuits; focus on the final grade and on mistakes made
Aggravated Accuracy Assessors	May choose to redo the same work over and over to try to make it more like their mind's ideal; may look frantically for ways to "fix" their work or find the necessary materials; may become disappointed and give up trying
Risk Evaders	Fear failure to achieve their standards and ideals due to asynchronous development or physical limitations; choose not to attempt the task
Controlling Image Managers	Want others to regard them as perfect; if they are afraid they are unable to meet expectations in competitive situations, they choose to eliminate themselves intentionally from the competition and say they could have been perfect if they wanted to compete
Procrastinating Perfectionists	Plan an extensive project but fail to start it for fear of their inability to achieve their perfect vision

Note. Information from Adelson (2007).

fectionism on three constructs: high standards, discrepancy (which is similar to evaluative concerns), and order (or having a desire for neatness in the environment). This scale also classifies perfectionism into healthy and unhealthy categories. The Clinical Perfectionism Questionnaire (Dickie et al., 2012) measures perfectionism on a single construct and is used by psychologists to identify **clinical perfectionism**, or perfectionism that has risen to the point of needing clinical interventions, such as therapy, in-patient treatment, or further diagnoses.

These types of instruments are used by researchers and professionals to study and to diagnose perfectionism. They are designed to be used by people who are trained in assessment procedures and familiar with research methodologies. Families are advised against using these instruments with their own children. Instead, interested families can contact professional psychologists or school personnel to administer assessments.

> *The instruments available to measure perfectionism reflect the theories held by the authors and developers of each test.*

Summary of Myth 4

Experts in the field of perfectionism have developed a wide variety of measures. These can be found throughout the journal articles and books that have been written about perfectionism that are listed in the references section of this book. These resources can be used to help identify children who may be in danger of developing perfectionism that affects their well-being. Again, the key is to identify manifestations of perfectionism and help students find healthier ways to think about goal attainment and achievement.

Myth 5: Perfectionism Is a Fixed Personality Trait

Many people who struggle with perfectionism assume that this trait cannot be changed. Families and educators who work with children who have perfectionism also often view this as a personality trait that remains stable over time and that is impervious to interventions. Is it true that "Once a perfectionist, always a perfectionist"?

If this were true, of course, there would be little point to us writing this book. However, we are also surprised about how pernicious and embedded this myth is in our society. How often have you heard, "I am such a perfectionist!" or seen the frustration of an educator or caregiver at the end of their rope with a child who struggles with perfectionism? It seems like, collectively, we have given up on trying to change perfectionistic habits of mind, and rather, accept perfectionism as an innate personality trait.

What the Research Says

A simple search of academic research articles about perfectionism from the last 10 years yielded more than 10,000 studies! That certainly kept these authors busy for a while, and in that stack of articles, many studies were conducted with young people and measured indicators of perfectionism at intervals (once a week, daily, or even several times a day). These studies found that perfectionistic tendencies and behavior vary within people across time. In other words, rather than being a stable trait, perfectionism varied depending on mood, context, and interventions (Dunkley, Berg, & Zuroff, 2012). Across the studies, feelings of loneliness, anxiety, depression, and worry were most associated with perfectionism (Chang, 2013; Handley et al., 2014; Huprich et al., 2008).

Additional research demonstrates that perfectionism is **domain-specific** (Stoeber & Stoeber, 2009), meaning that people tend to have perfectionistic tendencies or behaviors in particular areas of their life. For example, gifted children often focus their perfectionistic behaviors and tendencies on schoolwork, while elite athletes are perfectionistic toward their performance in their sport (Appleton et al., 2010). Thus, while participating in that activity, a person may score higher on a perfectionism scale than when involved in other aspects of their life.

We can better help children when we identify areas of life and times in which a child exhibits perfectionistic tendencies and behaviors rather than labeling the whole child as a perfectionist.

Summary of Myth 5

Rather than conceptualizing perfectionism as a personality trait that is innate and a core function of a person's being, it is more accurate to think of it as a state of mind that can change based upon the circumstances. For example, if a person is feeling more anxious, they are also likely to score higher on a perfectionism scale. Additionally, people tend to have perfectionism in specific areas of their life. Thus, we can better help children when we identify areas of life and times in which a child exhibits perfectionistic tendencies and behaviors rather than labeling the whole child as a perfectionist.

Myth 6: Adults Cannot Do Anything to Help Young Perfectionists

The frustration of families and educators dealing with perfectionistic behaviors and tendencies in children can be heard in almost any town, school, or neighborhood. Often, adults do not know where to turn or what to do to help their young children exhibiting perfectionistic tendencies and behaviors. The goal of adults is to change the negative aspects of perfectionism into healthier habits. Although perfectionism can be particularly resistant to change, researchers in psychology and education have developed strategies and interventions to help turn the tide of perfectionistic thoughts and to help children have positive motivation and realistic yet high goals.

What the Research Says

Research about interventions for perfectionism has primarily focused on group and individual therapies for **clinical perfectionism**. Quite a bit of success has been found with **cognitive behavioral therapy** in these settings (e.g., Radhu et al., 2012; Rozental et al., 2017). Cognitive behavioral therapy focuses on adjusting the negative thought patterns, assumptions, beliefs, evaluations, and behaviors of people into more positive and healthy outcomes. This therapy has been shown to reduce unhealthy perfectionistic tendencies and behaviors as well as depression and anxiety (Arpin-Cribbie et al., 2008).

Another strategy for addressing perfectionism in young children is **play therapy** (Ashby et al., 2004; Daigneault, 1999). Play therapy involves children in games and toys to help them cope with emotions and develop healthier patterns of behavior. Advocates of play therapy also suggest games that do not have a clear winner, such as the Ungame or Sleeping Grump (Ashby et al., 2004; see Chapter 11 for a description of these games).

> *If the child's perfectionism affects their health and well-being, be sure to seek professional help.*

Fewer studies have focused on the prevention of perfectionism for groups considered at-risk for developing perfectionistic behaviors. However, there have been some successes in whole-group activities and classroom interventions for gifted children who are already exhibiting some perfectionistic tendencies (e.g., Mofield & Chakraborti-Ghosh, 2010). For example, Aldea (2007) used an online forum to connect students with perfectionism and give them opportunities to reflect on their thought processes. Other online interventions have been effective when participants engaged in the online material (Egan et al., 2012).

Additionally, mindfulness techniques have been shown to be effective in individual and group therapy for both clinical (Wimberley et al., 2016) and nonclinical populations (Beck et al., 2017) to help reduce perfectionistic tendencies and behaviors. Techniques such as meditation, deep breathing, and focused thought are effective strategies for patients seeking treatment in clinical settings, as well as for others for whom perfectionism has not reached clinical levels. Some online resources for mindfulness are provided in Chapter 11.

Summary of Myth 6

Although many educators and families may still be searching for help with their perfectionistic children, there is help available. If the issues surrounding a child's perfectionism seem to be debilitating and interfering with a child's life, then professional help through psychologists or trained therapists is available. When families decide that professional intervention is appropriate, they should seek a licensed clinician to determine if the child is demonstrating clinical perfectionism. If so, there is the most research-based support for cognitive behavioral therapy for clinical perfectionism.

However, in this book, we are working on developing patterns of thoughts and behaviors that will help children and young adults modify tendencies *before* they reach clinical levels, that is, to overcome perfectionistic tendencies and behaviors and replace them with positive motivation and realistic, high goals. By using some of the strategies that we know have been successful in the past, educators and families can work to help children before they develop severe symptoms. Thus, techniques like mindfulness and introducing play can be preventative, and so can using curriculum that directly addresses perfectionism.

Myth 7: Perfectionism Is Not Really That Harmful for Children

Families and educators view perfectionism as a source of frustration for children, but they sometimes underestimate the seriousness of perfectionism. This can be particularly true for gifted children, who have such high capabilities that their perfectionism may seem to "pay off," or result in high achievement. Unhealthy manifestations of perfectionism often are seen as an issue that has only short-term, not long-term, consequences. Thus, families and educators sometimes ignore perfectionistic tendencies and behaviors in children, seeing them as a short-term and annoying problem. However, research suggests that unhealthy perfectionistic behaviors and tendencies may be closely associated with many more serious problems for children and young adults and can lead to more serious forms of psychological distress (Flett et al., 2016).

What the Research Says

Several studies have shown that perfectionism tends to increase over time (Curran & Hill, 2019; Kline & Short, 1991; Siegle & Schuler, 2000; Waller et al., 1992), indicating a need to intervene early to avoid later escalation of unhealthy behaviors and patterns of thought. The negative aspects of perfectionism have been documented in many studies as well and range from severe headaches (Kowal & Pritchard, 1990), social anxiety

(Biran & Reese, 2007; Gautreau et al., 2015; Laurenti et al., 2008), greater levels of anger (Öngen, 2009; Vallance et al., 2006), and poor health and greater alcohol consumption in college (Pritchard et al., 2007).

Children and adolescents who view perfection as the ideal goal often turn those expectations not only to academics, but also to their body image. Much of the research concerning unhealthy perfectionism is linked to eating disorders (Boone et al., 2012; Chang et al., 2008). Unhealthy perfectionism has been linked to greater severity of **anorexia** (Castro-Fornieles et al., 2007; Egan et al., 2012; Waller et al., 1992) and **bulimia** (Bardone-Cone, 2007; Castro-Fornieles et al., 2007; Downey & Chang, 2007; Esposito et al., 2019).

Early intervention is important to help children with perfectionistic tendencies change their behaviors and patterns of thought toward healthy motivation and realistic goals.

Perfectionism is often comorbid with **psychological distress**, suicidal ideation (Hewitt et al., 2014), and diagnoses, such as anxiety and depression (Handley et al., 2014; Hewitt et al., 2002; Huprich et al., 2008), obsessive-compulsive disorder (Boisseau et al., 2013), and borderline personality disorder (Dimaggio et al., 2018), often making the symptoms of these disorders more severe and more resistant to treatments (Limburg et al., 2017). Perfectionism also has been associated with symptoms of psychological distress, such as increased loneliness (Huprich et al., 2008), fatigue (Arpin-Cribbie & Cribbie, 2007), excessive worry (Chang et al., 2007), rumination (Flaxman et al., 2012), and lower life satisfaction (Gnilka et al., 2013).

Most seriously, perfectionism and the associated anxiety and depression can lead to suicide and suicidal thoughts in children and adolescents (O'Connor, 2007). Socially prescribed perfectionism and evaluative concerns perfectionism seem to be most identified with suicidal thoughts and suicide attempts (Blankstein et al., 2007; Boergers et al., 1998; Hewitt et al., 1997, 2014). Any mention of suicidal thoughts or indications of possible suicidal behavior should be brought to the attention of trained psychologists, counselors, or therapists, in any situation.

Summary of Myth 7

Perfectionism should not be taken lightly by families or educators. Although the symptoms may seem minor in early childhood, these behaviors and tendencies may escalate throughout the years and lead to more serious psychological consequences. These consequences may include anxiety, depression, and eating disorders. Educators and families can intervene when they see perfectionism having very negative, unhealthy effects on children and help guide children toward healthier cognitive processes and behaviors. When the symptoms lead to greater psychological distress or debilitating behaviors, families and educators should contact professional counselors, psychologists, or therapists for more intensive interventions.

Summary

Many families and educators hold misconceptions about perfectionism. Through a careful review of the relevant research concerning perfectionism and through other trustworthy sources, many of these myths can be dispelled. This chapter summarized the major research about perfectionism and provided information relevant to both families and educators concerning the children in their lives.

CHAPTER 3

The Academic Achiever

"Must Achieve 100%"

Caroline, a fourth grader, was a strong math student. Her teacher was working with her on sixth-grade mathematics content. She came home one night, and when her parents asked how her day at school was, she burst into tears. Once she calmed down, she explained that she had "failed a math test" and was too upset to explain. The next day, her parents stopped by the school to talk to Caroline's teacher. The test she had "failed" was a diagnostic test (a pretest). When they sat down with Caroline, she explained that she felt that she couldn't leave any answers blank—she had to know how to solve each problem or she wasn't smart in math. Despite the diagnostic nature of the assessment, Caroline struggled with the idea of skipping a problem and of struggling to solve a problem, whether she ever had been exposed to the concepts being tested or not.

Eric, another student talented in math, always came home and did his math homework first thing. He would do the assigned problems and then ask his parents to check them. If he missed even one due to a "careless" error, he believed he did not know the material well enough and would do numerous additional problems. Even after he had mastered a concept or skill, he often would continue to practice and feel insecure in his abilities because he did not do perfectly on the practice.

Shawanda's teacher had a policy that if the students misspelled no more than one word on the spelling pretest, then they did not have to take the test at the end of the week. However, when Shawanda missed a word, she came home upset at her performance and studied her words. Her parents assumed that she had to take the posttest because Shawanda studied the words and did the spelling homework every night. They did not realize that this was her own decision because she felt she was not perfect on the pretest.

Kalon's class was reviewing what they had learned over the course of the year in social studies in preparation for the state test. Although Kalon had a firm grasp of the concepts and key ideas that they had studied, he expected himself to remember every detail about each person, place, or event. During a review game, he knew the answer to the final question but did not remember exactly how it had been worded on his review sheet. He started pounding his head, trying to remember. Even after he won the game (and received credit for providing the correct answer to the final question), he sat frustrated with himself, trying to remember the precise wording.

Kwan's family moved from Korea to the United States when he was in kindergarten. Prior to that, Kwan had not been exposed to English. Later in elementary school, Kwan was identified for the self-contained gifted and talented class and worked very hard to earn top grades. He was particularly interested in mathematics and science, which came easily to him. By fourth grade, Kwan was reading above grade level. However, his grade in language arts was a low A. His parents worried about his reading ability and would request extra assignments for him. Moreover, Kwan was distraught about his language arts grade and believed he "wasn't good" at reading.

Blair loved to write poetry. She had been reading poetry since she had learned to read, and as a third grader she had several notebooks filled with her poems. During recess, she often would sit under the slide and write. When the PTA had an arts competition, Blair decided to write a poem for the entry. She worked every day on writing a poem to match the theme, and she finally had a poem she was happy with and excitedly submitted it. The day of the PTA program, she hopefully waited to hear the awards. However, she was crestfallen when they announced she had won second place. She went home after the program, threw away her notebooks, and told her parents she would never write a poem again because she was not good at it.

Academic Achievers are academically oriented students who exhibit negative perfectionism in their academic pursuits. They hold unrealistically high expectations for their own academic performance and expect perfection, and nothing less, from themselves. Typically, these students are high achievers with high grades, but they become disappointed with themselves when they earn anything less than what they perceive as a perfect score. They often are not satisfied with the achievements and grades they earn, wanting to earn all of the extra points and wanting to know (and earn) the highest possible score for each assessment. Even when they earn high grades, Academic Achievers are not satisfied with a "100" on an assignment or test, regularly completing extra credit projects and assignments with as much energy and effort as they put into their required work to score the maximum number of points possible.

Often, the identity of Academic Achievers lies in their academic achievements, and they see a mistake as a sign of failure and a flaw in their identity. Academic Achievers become very frustrated with themselves if they do not earn the top grade or cannot remember an answer word-for-word on every formal and informal assessment. Putting forth effort in their schoolwork typically is not an issue for Academic Achievers.

In fact, due to the extremely high standards that they impose on themselves, Academic Achievers often put forth more effort than required to master the material and achieve at the top level. Rather than a lack of effort being a problem, they sometimes have a problem with being too fixated on perfecting something rather than moving on to the next subject, problem, or challenge. Homework can be a struggle for these students, as they see every assessment—informal or formal, summative or formative—as an evaluation of their intelligence-identity and their self-worth. They do not see practice or homework as an opportunity to learn and to improve. Similarly, they have difficulty understanding the purpose of **diagnostic tests** and believe their inability to answer a question or to solve a problem means they are "not smart" or a failure. When taught a new concept or skill, Academic Achievers expect to immediately be proficient and demonstrate mastery without mistakes. They do not take pleasure in the struggles of a difficult problem and cannot experience the joy of an "Aha!" moment because they often become frustrated with themselves and give up easily when faced with a new academic challenge. They see the challenge not as an opportunity to grow and learn but as a testament to their own failure and flaws.

> *Academic Achievers often have identities tightly tied to their academic achievement. Thus, imperfect achievement at school may lead to* **imposter syndrome.**

Another issue for Academic Achievers is their tendency to focus heavily on their mistakes. Even when they meet the expectations of the task at hand, these students, unfortunately, rarely are satisfied with their performance. Rather than looking at the progress or the process, Academic Achievers are focused on the end product, particularly on the evaluation of that product (typically a grade), and they judge themselves on that criterion alone. They might come home and express to their families that they "failed" a test because it was challenging or because they earned a low A or a B. They fixate on imperfect grades on a report card or on the handful of questions they may have missed on a test. Because their identity is tied to their academic achievements, if they are in an academic competition, including review games in the classroom, they can become distraught and believe they are "dumb" if they do not win. Missing one question out of a hundred might result in crumpled papers and tears rather than satisfaction in correctly answering 99% of the questions or in improving from the previous test. For Academic Achievers, mistakes are glaring, and success is defined by perfection.

> *Academic Achievers are overly focused on their mistakes and not their successes and mastery of concepts.*

Although the pressure for perfect work often is internal for Academic Achievers, who tie their identity to their academic achievements, this pressure also can arise from the expectations of family and peers. In some cases, like that of Kwan, family pressures feed the Academic Achiever's stress on themselves for perfection. A parent's focus on doing well academically and on achieving specific grades might fuel an Academic Achiever's own internal pressure to do well. Additionally, being referred to as "the smart one" in a family or group, or being consistently praised for being smart and getting all A's, might create further tension in the Academic Achiever because it solidifies the academically oriented identity that is tied to the child's outcomes rather than process or progress. The label of "gifted" or being pulled out for special programs may create a similar atmosphere for students. This internal identity for the Academic Achiever often is furthered by comments made by caregivers, siblings, other relatives, peers, or educators. Although these people may not be disappointed with less than perfection, Academic Achievers might believe they are letting these people down if they make academic mistakes or admit to not knowing something.

Strategies for the Classroom

Because the Academic Achiever's identity is so tied to their academic achievement, it is essential that educators are aware of these students in their classrooms. Although it is easy and quite natural for educators and families alike to praise students for high grades, it is more important to praise students, particularly Academic Achievers, for their efforts and progress. Rather than focusing on "being smart" and earning good grades, you need to place significantly more emphasis on the effort and **problem-solving strategies** of Academic Achievers. This becomes a model for students, but it is not enough. Academic Achievers need guidance from their educators in how to take pride in the process and how to use mistakes as learning experiences. **Diagnostic assessments**, or tests used at the beginning of units of study to determine the knowledge students already possess on a topic, are not only tools for acceleration and compacting, but also good tools for working with Academic Achievers. These types of assessment can teach them not to expect perfection on everything academic in nature, teaching them that assessments can be formative as well as summative. For example, after Caroline's teacher worked with her on identifying areas of strengths and weaknesses, she learned the purpose of diagnostic testing and learned to take tests with less anxiety, eagerly helping to pinpoint the content and skills she did not know.

Successful Strategies for the Classroom

- Praise efforts and progress.
- Use diagnostic testing and focus on growth.
- Use formative assessment as a tool to teach learning from mistakes.
- Use portfolios and reflection to help students recognize strengths.
- Incorporate practice on students' weaknesses into topics or areas of strength.

Academic Achievers are focused on summative evaluation and on the final grade, without an eye toward learning from mistakes. In addition to using formative assessment for your own purposes, you also should use it as an opportunity to guide students in learning from their mistakes and recognizing their own mastery. To help Eric focus more on learning from his mistakes rather than only despairing at his imperfections, his teacher asked him to correct his mistakes and write **WIMI (Why I Missed It**; see Chapter 9) statements. This approach removed the emphasis from "less than 100%" to learning from mistakes and recognizing reasons Eric incorrectly solved problems. Eric came to recognize that mastery and perfection were not equivalent and that practice helps people learn from mistakes but does not need to be perfect.

Similarly, once Shawanda's parents met with her teacher and realized what Shawanda was doing, they worked with her on not penalizing herself for not being perfect. Rather than focusing on the entire list during the week, Shawanda's teacher would allow her to spell the one word she missed during the posttest, focusing the attention on learning from her pretest and accepting mastery of the other words. After a few weeks, Shawanda realized that when she misspelled a word, she still had mastered the list for that week, and she no longer participated in the posttest. Instead, she would study words from a challenge list so that she could compete in the district spelling bee later that year.

In addition to learning from their mistakes, Academic Achievers need to learn to recognize their improvement and progress rather than basing their evaluation on a final grade or assessment. For Kalon, who was so focused on achievement that he had to remember everything word-for-word, seeing his growth in understanding helped him not be so hard on himself and have such unrealistic expectations. At the beginning of a unit, Kalon's teacher had him create a concept map showing what he already knew about the topic. As part of his final assessment, Kalon created another concept map or mind map to demonstrate his additional learning. Comparing the two, Kalon had a visual representation that allowed him to see that he truly had learned a lot and to focus more on concepts rather than precise wording. For Blair, whose focus was on the final evaluation, her teacher worked with her on critiquing her poetry that she submitted to competitions and keeping a poetry portfolio. In her critique, Blair learned to identify the strengths of her poetry, as well as look at it from the eye of a judge to determine what could be improved. More than that, with each submission, Blair took some time to review her portfolio and list improvements in her poetry. This helped her enjoy competitions more, as she could take pride in her improvements, which were under her control, rather than focus on how she did in comparison to others.

Recognizing improvement and progress sometimes is not enough. Some Academic Achievers, like Kwan, are so focused on their weaknesses that they do not recognize, much less celebrate, their strengths. Kwan continued to work on his language arts skills, but his teacher worked with him to move the focus from the grade to improvement, keeping a portfolio and reflecting on progress throughout the year. Rather than focusing solely on his "weakness" and comparing it to the abilities of his peers, Kwan needed to begin recognizing his strengths. His teacher met with him at the beginning of each marking period to discuss his strengths, his improvements, and what he would like to achieve during the next marking period. Moreover, she used recommended best practices and helped Kwan address his "weakness" through his strengths—incorporating more reading and writing in Kwan's mathematics and science assignments, which piqued his interest and helped him to improve.

Strategies for the Home

Families of Academic Achievers often find themselves in awkward situations. On one hand, they are pleased with their child's commitment to academic success, but on the other hand, they are troubled by their child's sometimes unhealthy obsession with perfection in academic tasks. It may be difficult for caregivers to find support from other caregiviers or school personnel and resources for their situation.

One step that you can take is to focus family goals less on grades and more on academic learning. This may be accomplished through careful observation of the words used with children when discussing school. For example, you may ask what the child learned from a project or from a unit of study, rather than what grade they obtained on the final product or chapter test. You may even want to avoid looking at report cards and grades in front of your child, focusing instead on listening to your child discuss their learning and accomplishments. If your child already is aware of their grades, then, in most situations, it is unnecessary for you to place additional emphasis on grades. Instead, you should focus on areas that your child improved and also talk about strategies for your child to improve any areas that they are not pleased with.

Successful Strategies for the Home

- Deemphasize grades.
- Celebrate learning and growth.
- Be an example in your mistakes.
- Choose books and movies to illustrate **"flawed protagonists."**
- Find off-peak times to talk to your child.

Instead of focusing on the teacher's and others' evaluations of student achievement, you should celebrate your child's learning and growth. Family dinners, car rides to and from school activities, and other moments provide excellent opportunities to discuss with your child their achievements for the day that are separated from others' evaluations of those activities. You can work with your child during these times to feel pride in learning a new skill in math rather than focusing their pride on an A on the final test. The goal here is to move your child from relying on **extrinsic rewards**, such as grades, to **intrinsic rewards**, such as the feeling of accomplishment from learning a new skill.

To extend this idea, your family may wish to have a celebration at the end of each unit of study, grading period, or semester to recognize the accomplishments of each family member. These accomplishments should not be external evaluations of accomplishment. Rather, they should focus on the growth and learning that took place during the time period. One family, for example, ordered pizza and had ice cream at the end of each grading period. During the course of the meal, each family member, adults included, shared the area in which they felt they had learned the most during the 6-week time period. Another family chose to celebrate each time a family member completed a significant project. This celebration occurred before feedback from the teacher or supervisor was given, keeping the focus on the accomplishment that the family member felt at completing the task. This helped to emphasize the internal rewards of working hard at a project rather than the external evaluation from others. Additionally, if your child has taken a pre- and posttest on a topic, you can use that to help your child recognize and celebrate growth made during the course of a unit of study.

When struggling with an Academic Achiever, many families look to biographies, books, and movies for examples that show a healthy balance of success and failures. Even notable figures did not perform perfectly on every occasion. Albert Einstein missed key questions on his college entrance exams. And, although Mary Lou Retton won the gold all-around medal in the 1984 Olympics, she only won the bronze on the floor exercise. There are many lists of biographies that are suitable for this purpose (e.g., Hébert, 1991, 2020). Rhuday-Perkovich's (2020) list includes people from diverse backgrounds (see https://www.readbrightly.com/illustrated-biographies-that-introduce-kids-to-diverse-heroes). Children also may wish to research their own heroes and heroines to find out about not only their successes, but also times when they were less than perfect.

Educators are familiar with the term *teachable moment*, in which an unexpected event in the classroom provides an excellent opportunity to extend student learning. As a caregiver, you can look for similar moments when you are with your children, whether they are watching TV, going to the movies, or reading the news. Characters in sitcoms often make mistakes, but part of the lesson of the show is for the character to admit their mistake and move on. This type of situation may need to be emphasized to children and talked about in a family discussion. Families also can observe their children's interactions with other children carefully; peer interactions can offer multiple teaching moments to apply simple situations like board games or craft projects to the idea of general improvement or completion of a task, as opposed to being the best or winning in a competitive situation.

> *The most important tool for families is communication with their children.*

In addition to **teachable moments**, many families find success talking with children about delicate situations, such as perfectionism, during "off-peak times." **Off-peak times** are times when the situation is not immediately pressing and both the child and adults are calm. For example, you may experience more success in talking with your child about perfectionism not when your child is in the middle of a breakdown but at a time when your child is not necessarily thinking about schoolwork, such as on the ride home from soccer practice or while cuddling up with a good book at bedtime.

Although the families of Academic Achievers often find the situation overwhelming and frustrating, there are several strategies that may help their child have a healthy balance of academic endeavors, as noted in this section. The most important tool for families is communication with their children. By communicating about expectations and how you define learning and success, you can help your child set reasonable academic goals and standards and focus on growing as a learner.

Final Thoughts

Academic Achievers hold themselves to unrealistically high expectations in academic endeavors. They easily can become fixated on anything less than a perfect score. They do not see the goals of education as being to improve, to learn, and to master new content and skills. Instead, they expect to know everything on the first attempt and see all academic activities as something they must complete flawlessly. Families and educators of Academic Achievers can work with them to change their unrealistic expectations into realistic goals, focusing on personal growth rather than perfection.

CHAPTER 4

The Aggravated Accuracy Assessor

"Exactness and Fixation on 'Redos'"

Ivan exhibited artistic talent at a young age. He was particularly talented at drawing portraits, creating realistic drawings that were quite precise given his age (fourth grade) and still-developing fine motor skills. The fourth graders were creating paintings for a Virginia studies art gallery in their school, and Ivan had decided to draw a Civil War soldier. During several art classes, Ivan meticulously worked on his drawing. He would tune out all of his classmates and be completely absorbed in the fine details of his drawing. His concentration was broken by only one thing—he constantly would get up and take the drawing to the art teacher and his classroom teacher for reassurance that it was "good." Every time Ivan's drawing neared completion, he would decide to redo the drawing because it

37

was not precise enough. He would see some detail that was not just right and crumple up the drawing, starting over.

By the time children are in upper elementary school, they are beginning to learn to take notes in class. Many students appreciate this opportunity to use shorthand, to not worry so much about handwriting, and to not be expected to create a "final copy." However, Leta dreaded any time she had to take notes in class because she just did not have enough time for preciseness. In fifth grade, Leta's social studies teacher was working with the students on different note-taking strategies, and her class was followed immediately by recess. Each day that they worked on note-taking, when the other students excitedly went out to play, Leta would ask to stay and continue writing or copying her notes. She would painstakingly write each individual letter of every word, taking extra time and putting forth extra effort to ensure that her notes were as neat as possible. If given the opportunity, Leta would rewrite her notes, not as a method of learning the material but because she was frustrated at how "messy" they were. At times, Leta would fall behind in another class because she was fixated on rewriting her notes or finishing her notes and could not mentally or physically move on to another subject. Her mom found her homework taking her much longer than would be expected at this age and realized that Leta was bringing her notebooks home and recopying everything, sometimes erasing so many times to make each individual letter perfect that she would rip a hole in the paper, creating a meltdown because she then had to start all over again. Her mother often was left bewildered and frustrated as a result of Leta's meltdowns.

Devon, a third grader, was interested in architecture. From a young age, he had been fascinated with the different types of buildings related to the cultures and time periods his teachers would introduce to the class. When studying ancient Egypt, he decided to build a replica of a pyramid. He carefully researched the architecture and design of the interior, the dimensions, the materials, and all other aspects of the Great Pyramids before he began gathering his materials and creating his pyramid. He would spend several hours working on the pyramid, make substantial progress, and then decide that some angle was not "just right" or a dimension was too short or too long, and he would start all over. The school's open house took place almost one month after Devon had started building his pyramid. His parents came and saw the projects that Devon's classmates had been working on and mostly had finished. However, when they asked Devon where his pyramid was, he showed them the plans for his pyramid. He did not have anything built at that point because he had, once again, decided to start over from the beginning.

Andy had been skateboarding almost as long as he had been walking. He loved the sport and would spend as much time as possible at the local skate park. He was in fifth grade, and he already was competing in skate contests and holding his own against competitors 4 to 7 years older than him. He would watch videos of professional skaters like Tony Hawk and Bob Burnquist, memorizing every trick that they did. Andy's favorite trick was the Ollie 540, and he would use his TV's slow-motion capability to watch the skaters' form and movements as they completed the trick. However, he could not do the trick himself. He would spend hours, until well past exhaustion, working on the same move over and over. One problem that Andy had was that he was going through a growth spurt and was experiencing awkward coordination as he grew into his body. He also had yet to master some of the skills leading up to this level of trick. Despite these limitations, he insisted he knew how to do the trick and refused to stop practicing it, often to the detriment of his schoolwork and the development of other skateboarding skills.

Radhika loved the piano. She had been playing for several years and thoroughly enjoyed both competing and practicing. Her parents did not have to encourage her to practice—she did so on her own, often longer than her instructor had suggested she had to each day. On more than one occasion, Radhika would turn down an invitation to play with her friends because she was in the middle of practicing. Radhika had chosen a particularly difficult piece to play for an upcoming concert. Although she had picked the piece well in advance, the concert was only a week away, and she still had not played the piece all of the way through. Radhika would get a little way into the piece, make an error—whether playing a wrong key, holding a note too long, or even forgetting to change volumes immediately—and would get frustrated and start again from the beginning. She refused to continue the song after making any mistake; therefore, she had yet to practice the second half of the song at all. In her lessons, the instructor

sometimes would not even hear the error, but Radhika would stop, frustrated with herself for not being perfect. When pushed to continue, she would become so perturbed about not being perfect that she would lose her concentration and fumble through the rest of the song, often bringing herself to tears. At one point, she declared she just could not do it anymore and refused to play the rest of the song.

Trisha had been working on her tessellation project for her mathematics class for 2 weeks. Her mom had asked her several times to see her work, but Trisha always told her it wasn't ready yet. Whenever her mom came to her room while she was working on the tessellation, Trisha would quickly hide her work. She kept telling her mom that she had to fix it, that it wasn't just right yet, and that she would show her when it was perfect. The night before the project was due, Trisha's mom again asked to see the project. Trisha again said it wasn't ready and asked if she could start over. When her mom explained that it was getting late and the project was due the next day, Trisha frantically searched for a large eraser and correction fluid and ran back to her room. Her mom found her in there trying to edit her work completely. When she asked Trisha what she was doing, Trisha explained that she just had to fix it—no matter what she did, she couldn't make her tessellation look "right."

Mr. Troy was teaching his second graders about area. To help them with the concept of covering a space, he had the students measure the area of different surfaces by covering them with sheets of scrapbook paper that were one square foot. They had already discussed the need to line up the squares so that there were no gaps or overlaps. As the students worked in groups to measure several surfaces, Mr. Troy noticed that although most groups were on their third or fourth surface, his highest ability group was still on the first one. He went over to listen to their conversation and see what was happening. While Erin sat back and watched, both Darius and Vivian were carefully aligning the squares. If the squares were even slightly off, they would go back and rearrange them. Given that the rug they were trying to measure was 32 square feet, this was quite time consuming. Every time a couple of new squares were placed, Darius or Vivian would see a square that was not precisely lined up, go readjust it, and then have to readjust every other square based on that change. Mr. Troy wondered if they would ever finish even the first part of this classroom activity.

Precision and perfection are the goals for **Aggravated Accuracy Assessors**. They do not take pride in the process but focus completely on the end product. Any deviation from their plan or from the "rules" creates a desperate need to repair what they are doing. They become very aggravated with themselves for not being able to do a task exactly right, and they spend inordinate lengths of time redoing or refining, often at the detriment of other areas of their lives. Aggravated Accuracy Assessors often have difficulty with goal setting, as the only goal worthwhile in their mind is perfection, and they become so focused on creating one particular flawless work or perfecting one particular skill that they cannot divert any of their energy or attention to anything else.

> *Aggravated Accuracy Assessors are overly focused on precision and on a flawless final product, not enjoying or taking pride in the process.*

The unhealthy perfectionistic behaviors exhibited by Aggravated Accuracy Assessors may result from **asynchronous development**, which is a hardship faced by many perfectionists who are gifted and talented (Miller et al., 2012; Morelock, 1992; Silverman, 1993a, 1993b; Tannenbaum, 1992). Gifted children's minds may develop faster than their bodies, especially when physical skills are involved, such as in art, music, and sports. Aggravated Accuracy Assessors experiencing asynchronous development often attempt the tasks but become frustrated with their inability to meet their mind's ideal. They have a perfect image in their mind, and they understand the intricacies of the discipline, field, or product, yet the final product does not meet their high standards. Aggravated Accuracy Assessors constantly evaluate their products and progress and become aggravated and discouraged by their efforts and products. Often, these children will redo the same piece of work or process over and over again in an effort to make it match their mind's ideal. They may hide their works in progress, not wanting others to see their imperfect work or to offer critiques of it. If pushed to finish a piece of work, they may frantically try to "fix" it or may become so disappointed in their work and themselves that they give up entirely.

Perfectionism is a trait that children and adults alike exhibit in a variety of areas, not just in school. These areas can include art, music, and sports. Although a child may tend to exhibit perfectionistic tendencies in multiple areas, some adults are surprised to find that a child who is perfectionistic in one area can be "sloppy" or not detail- or goal-oriented in another area. Several of the Aggravated Accuracy Assessors described here fall into this category. For instance, Andy's grades were falling because he was so focused on his skateboarding, and Radhika, who exhibited perfectionism in her piano playing and also in her academic achievements, did not display these same attitudes toward her softball practice or keeping her room tidy. Although Andy and Radhika both were very focused on being perfect in a particular domain and spent hours refining their skills, they did not apply this same attention to detail to other areas of their lives. In fact, they were so focused on being perfect in their chosen domain that they often did not spend the necessary time to meet others' standards in other areas. To them, nothing else mattered besides being flawless at the particular skill on which they were focused.

> *Perfectionism may affect a child in numerous areas of life, including academics, sports, and art. It may be focused on a specific domain or more general and pervasive.*

Sometimes, Aggravated Accuracy Assessors are not focused on a particular long-term product or skill but find that their perfectionism affects many tasks at home and at school, such as Darius and Vivian trying to measure the area of a surface and Leta taking notes. Although they did not focus on a project like Devon's pyramid or a skill like Andy's Ollie 540, these students were just as focused on redoing and repairing the task at hand to achieve perfection. Although the stakes may not be as high as with long-term projects, these students are just as invested in being perfect and become just as aggravated with themselves if they do not achieve perfection.

Strategies for the Classroom

Creating high-quality products and improving their processes are goals we do not want to discourage our children from. But we do want to help them use their intrinsic motivation and set goals in a healthy way, rather than being overly aggravated with themselves, giving up on their goal, or fixating on one project—all unhealthy, perfectionistic behaviors. Therefore, it is essential to help Aggravated Accuracy Assessors recognize that their standards are acceptable and valuable as **long-term goals**. As an educator, you must have faith in your students' vision and their ability to meet their own expectations through effort and revision. This support is key for Aggravated Accuracy Assessors before you can begin helping them modify their immediate standards or goals. By reframing students' unrealistic **short-term goals**, or immediate goals, as long-term goals, you are helping them become more realistic in their expectations and more likely to experience success. Additionally, Aggravated Accuracy Assessors may need to hold conferences with you and their caregivers about their progress in school and at home, particularly if their focus on one goal is harming their progress in other domains.

Successful Strategies for the Classroom

- Recognize students' standards as acceptable as long-term goals requiring effort and revision.
- Help students reframe unrealistic short-term goals as long-term goals.
- Discuss and celebrate success as a result of revision.
- Focus on process and improvement rather than final product.
- Create a safe environment for critiquing work.
- Provide opportunities for practice and imperfection as well as to showcase final products.

Aggravated Accuracy Assessors have difficulty seeing the benefits of the revision process because they are so focused on the end product. They, like most students, could benefit from reading about and discussing successful people who have revised their works numerous times. You should engage students frustrated with their writing or the writing process in a discussion about the following quote by Avi, who wrote *The True Confessions of Charlotte Doyle* and *Nothing but the Truth*: "I enjoy writing and it is hard. But then it is hard for everyone to write well. I have to rewrite over and over again so that on average it takes me a year to write a book" (IPL, 1996).

Students struggling to invent, create, or build something might read about Thomas Edison, who spent almost 2 years and tried more than 6,000 different carbonized plant fibers before inventing a successful light bulb, or they might read about Formula 409, which is named after the fact that the successful kitchen-cleaning formula was the 409th attempt of two young scientists from Detroit, MI. Many students, like Ivan, struggle in art, and they would benefit from learning about examples of famous artists' works, revisions, biographies, and autobiographies that illustrate the amount of time devoted to their masterpieces. In particular, Leonardo da

Vinci's "failed" artistic experiments may show children that even famous artists do not always get it perfect. Da Vinci's masterpiece *The Last Supper* literally began to flake off the wall even during his lifetime due to the failed experiment of developing new types of paints. One of the first responses to Louisa May Alcott's manuscript of *Little Women* was "stick to teaching," but she persevered, her book became a bestseller, and it is now considered a classic. Perhaps African American writer and artist Faith Ringgold said it best when describing how she uses history to inspire change for the future: "I like to turn wrong into right in a positive way" (Elderton, 2020).

Moreover, Aggravated Accuracy Assessors who experience asynchronous development that affects their physical ability to meet their mind's ideal need to be exposed to the body of work of artists to see that skills are built over time and that success is not always immediate. It took years for Vincent van Gogh to develop his rich, expressive style and bold use of color and brushstrokes. Similarly, Pablo Picasso experimented with many different art styles before inventing Cubism. Many examples of artists' early work can be found in books, museums, and even online. Educators can use units of study on art history or particular art movements as teachable moments for offering insight on the need for growth and improvement over time, emphasizing that many famous artists did not get their works "right" the first time.

Focusing on the process and on improvement is a way to help students not be consumed by the final product. Moreover, Aggravated Accuracy Assessors need to realize that even the "final" product can be a work in progress and that every project is an opportunity to learn and improve. You should provide your students opportunities to critique their peers' work, indicating aspects that they admire and offering constructive suggestions for improvement. You can redirect criticism of a student's work as well. For example, in looking at a student like Leta, who focuses on perfection in neatness, you could emphasize how much you like her creative ideas and encourage her to share more creativity with you. Creating a safe environment where students can discuss their works in progress and final works, whether it be writing, art, a project like Devon's pyramid, or a physical skill like piano or skateboarding, helps students begin to see what they have done successfully as well as set future goals based on what they have accomplished. As students learn to examine their own work, you should encourage them to identify not only weaknesses, which Aggravated Accuracy Assessors are used to focusing on, but also strengths. When looking at the weaknesses, Aggravated Accuracy Assessors need guidance in setting goals to improve those weaknesses and look at them as opportunities for progress and advancement rather than as faults.

When the Aggravated Accuracy Assessors' attention to detail derails them from participating in class discussion and activities, such as with Leta who was overly focused on perfect handwriting, these students need help **prioritizing**. Especially at the elementary school level, when students are still learning and practicing their handwriting, students may not realize that there is a difference between "perfect" and "legible" or that perfect handwriting is not necessary in every situation. You must guide these students to help them distinguish between those times when handwriting is more important and those when it just needs to be legible. One strategy is to have students create "sloppy copies" without any erasing. You can have them write with a pen or with a pencil without an eraser. Students should write as they think, crossing or scribbling out, writing above and below lines, and drawing arrows. Some students might enjoy learning conventional editing and revising marks. This gives students permission not to assess their accuracy during the draft period, focusing more on their ideas and the content. Take the time to call attention to your own revising process and less-than-perfect handwriting skills when jotting down ideas and notes. However, you must recognize the needs of Aggravated Accuracy Assessors to work on doing their best, including their handwriting. In addition to the "sloppy copies," students also need opportunities to use their "perfect" handwriting and to publish the work. When students are working on their final copies, you should work with them to recognize that although they will want their final copy to be neat and presentable, they do not have to create a perfect final piece. Help them to focus on the substance of their writing rather than just its appearance. Some children respond well to the suggestion that irregularities in a final copy give it a personal touch. For other students, the opportunity to complete their final copy on the computer may help alleviate anxiety about making mistakes. This same process can be used for other domains, such as art. Sketching and doodling should be encouraged, including strategies such as "sketchnotes," as well as final products. Improvisation and sight reading may be highlighted in music lessons, along with polished compositions.

Strategies for the Home

Families of Aggravated Accuracy Assessors often become as frustrated as their children with the need for perfection. These feelings of frustration often come to a head when both caregivers and children are at the heights of aggravation. As a caregiver, you should make every effort to help your child cope with these feelings before they escalate.

One strategy is to help children set goals in multiple areas of their life. These goals should include not only academic goals, but also social, extracurricular, and personal or self-improvement goals. The emphasis should be on a **well-balanced life** that includes many facets of a child's life. For example, in addition to improvement in spelling, a child also may add spending time playing games with friends, keeping their room tidier, and improving accuracy when shooting the basketball to their list of goals. Notice that these are **personal goals**, focused on what the child wants to improve, master, and enjoy, rather than competitive goals, like winning a competition or sport.

Another strategy when defining goals with children is to help them distinguish between realistic and unrealistic goals. Attaining perfection in all areas of life is an unrealistic goal, but improving spelling scores is a realistic goal. It is not realistic for children to expect that they would not make any mistakes when recopying class notes, but it is realistic to use a computer to help type them in a neater fashion.

Finally, goals should be classified as short-, medium-, or long-term goals. This may help children realize that although a goal may be worthwhile, it will not always happen in an immediate time frame. For example, Andy's goal of completing the skateboarding trick could have been a medium- or long-term goal. He needed time to develop his skills in other areas before he was ready to try the Ollie 540. Ivan could have developed a short-term goal to complete the Civil War drawing, while making a long-term goal to draw a portrait realistically. This may help to relieve some of the pressure that these children tend to place upon themselves.

Successful Strategies for the Home

- Help children set goals in multiple areas of life.
- Distinguish between realistic and unrealistic goals.
- Distinguish between short-, medium-, and long-term goals.
- Model mistakes.
- Encourage children to realize their own limitations.
- Discuss problems of asynchrony.
- Help children prioritize.

In the discussions of goal setting, it often is important to have children recognize their own limitations. For example, a child might be able to say, "If I had all night to work on this project, I might be able to make it more perfect, but it is healthier for me to get a good night's sleep." This skill may take some time for children to develop, and families may have to engage their children in multiple discussions before children are able to verbalize this themselves. It is important, however, for children to give themselves permission to be less than perfect.

In discussions of limitations, it may be helpful for families to bring up issues of asynchronous development. Children may experience the frustration of the limitations from their fine motor skills or other areas of development, without the knowledge or ability to express this frustration. Explaining that a child's intellect or brain may develop faster than their body may help to relieve some of this anxiety. For our own children, understanding these developmental differences has helped them come to terms with the differences between their achievements and their expectations.

When discussing limitations of time, it may help to have children begin to prioritize their obligations and responsibilities. Creating a **pie chart**, divided into 24 hours, may help children begin to realize how detrimental obsession in one aspect of their lives can be to other areas (see Figure 1). By realizing that when they unnecessarily spend hours on one homework activity, they are missing out on other activities that they enjoy, children may be able to better prioritize their lives. Working with your child, you can help to set limits on the amount of time that should be spent on one activity, such as note-taking.

When organizing how time should be spent with your child, several techniques may be helpful. A daily or weekly calendar can be a visual for students to see how they should divide their time. We have included a

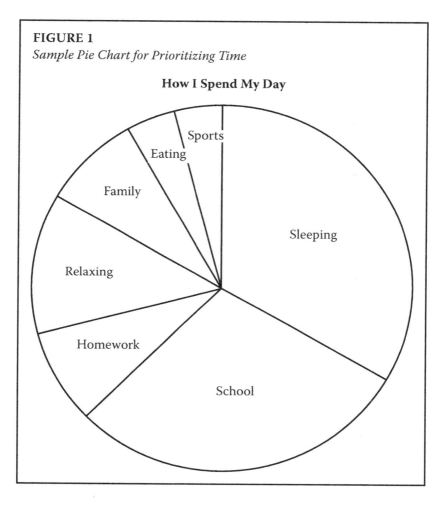

FIGURE 1
Sample Pie Chart for Prioritizing Time

How I Spend My Day

sample calendar and a blank calendar to organize children's time (see Figures 2 and 3). To keep track of the time during the afternoon or evening, many families find the use of a kitchen timer helpful. However, for some children, this creates an additional layer of anxiety. Instead of using a timer, it may be more effective to give gentle reminders to your child, such as, "You have about 15 more minutes to work on that," and count down at 5-minute intervals. This prepares your child to end the activity and gives them assistance in managing their time.

Finally, you can work to serve as a role model for your child's activities. You may want to point out, for example, that although having a spotless

FIGURE 2
Sample Calendar

	Monday	Tuesday	Wednesday	Thursday	Friday
3:00	Snack	Snack	Snack	Snack	Snack
3:30	Homework	Homework	Homework	Homework	Project/Study Time
4:00	Project/Study Time	Project/Study Time	Project/Study Time	Project/Study Time	Fun Reading
4:30	Flex Time*	Flex Time*	Flex Time*	Flex Time*	Flex Time*
5:00	Piano Lessons	*Free Time*	Soccer	*Free Time*	*Free Time*
5:30	Piano Lessons	Fun Reading	Soccer	*Free Time*	*Free Time*
6:00	Dinner	Dinner	Dinner	Dinner	Dinner
6:30	Dinner/Chores	Dinner/Chores	Dinner/Chores	Dinner/Chores	Dinner/Chores
7:00	*Free Time*	Family Games	*Free Time*	Attend Sis's Game	Friends
7:30	*Free Time*	Family Games	*Free Time*	Attend Sis's Game	Friends
8:00	Fun Reading	Family Games	Fun Reading	Fun Reading	Friends
8:30	Bedtime	Bedtime	Bedtime	Bedtime	Bedtime

Note. "Flex time" is to be used to finish homework, work on ongoing projects, or study as necessary. If all work is caught up, then this is free time.

FIGURE 3
Blank Calendar

	Monday	Tuesday	Wednesday	Thursday	Friday
3:00					
3:30					
4:00					
4:30					
5:00					
5:30					
6:00					
6:30					
7:00					
7:30					
8:00					
8:30					

house is an important goal for you, there are still dust bunnies in the corners of the living room because it was more important to fix dinner and spend time with the family. Teachable moments in your own life may serve as excellent examples for your child's behaviors.

Although coping with an Aggravated Accuracy Assessor can be frustrating for both you and your child, strategies within the home can help to alleviate many of the stressors. You should work carefully with your child to set goals, prioritize time, and serve as a role model for managing multiple activities.

Final Thoughts

Aggravated Accuracy Assessors spend much of their time fixing their mistakes and are focused primarily on the end product. They do not understand that there are times when perfection is not expected and when being meticulous can be detrimental. The smallest perceived flaw can create panic for Aggravate Accuracy Assessors, and they obsess over each little detail. Educators and families can help these students by emphasizing the importance of the process of getting to the end product and assisting the child in making realistic goals. This might include breaking larger long-term goals into **subtasks**, helping create timelines, discussing priorities, and providing opportunities for "sloppy copies" and for polished final copies. Examples of worksheets that caregivers and children can complete together are shown in Figures 4 and 5. These worksheets can help adults and children work to develop goals and plans for meeting those goals. In subsequent chapters, you can find more resources for planning specific projects with children.

FIGURE 4
Goals Worksheet

Area of Life	Goal/ Priority	Steps to Accomplish	Check *(When Completed)*
Social			
Family			
Physical			
Academic			
Activities			

FIGURE 5
Priorities Worksheet

Area of Life	Specific Priority	Rank
Social		
Family		
Physical		
Academic		
Activities		
Other:		

CHAPTER 5

The Risk Evader

"All or Nothing"

Mrs. Gonzalez, the art teacher, had taught many students and was always excited when she saw an elementary student with emerging talent. One of the students with natural artistic ability was Elena. Mrs. Gonzalez had complimented her since first grade on her artwork, which consistently was above the level of detail and accuracy of her peers. Elena had a particular talent for realistic drawings, especially as her fine motor skills developed in the later elementary years. Mrs. Gonzalez had talked to Elena about her talent and had complimented her drawings in class. In fifth grade, all students were required to submit a piece of artwork for a schoolwide contest, and Elena won the overall award, receiving many accolades from the judges. However, although Elena happily drew in her notebook in the privacy of her room at home and at school during lunch and recess, she did not want to participate in drawing in art class or in art competitions. She reluctantly drew in art class, dreading the appraisal that would or would not come. Despite encouragement from her parents, classroom teacher, and art teacher, she refused to enter her artwork from the schoolwide contest into the district contest. Elena did not want to risk what others would say about her artwork or that she might not win. Mrs. Gonzalez and Elena's parents lamented her decision and the missed opportunities.

Jacob really enjoyed singing and always had fun participating in the school PTA performances. He looked forward to his grade's turn to perform every year. In fourth grade, he had his heart set on a major role in the musical. His music teacher, Mrs. Lee, had commented to his mom that he had strong singing abilities for his age and should be able to earn that role. Unfortunately, Jacob became ill shortly before the tryouts, leaving him with little voice or energy on audition day. Understandably, Jacob chose not to try out that day, afraid that his illness

would prevent him from performing at his best and earning him the role. His teacher talked with him and suggested he request an audition on another day, but Jacob refused to do so. Although he had told all of his friends he would earn that role, his confidence had been shaken, and he did not want to risk not being selected as the lead, even if there were other roles he also might enjoy playing.

Prairiethorpe Elementary School's academic team competed at several tournaments throughout the year. The students would study trivia and would meet for practices about twice a week. At the beginning of each semester, the coach, one of the fifth-grade teachers, would hold tryouts for the team. Lizzie's older brother had been on the team, and she had been excited about trying out since she first entered Prairiethorpe. Lizzie knew lots of trivia, and her classmates and family assumed she would get on the team. Tryout day came, and Lizzie got in line to get on the bus as usual. Her teacher knew that Lizzie would be a good addition to the team and was surprised to see her in the bus line and not headed to the tryouts. Lizzie told her that she had to go home and her mom would not let her stay. Later that month at parent-teacher conferences, Lizzie's mom commented on how disappointed Lizzie had been not to be on the academic team, and her teacher responded that it was a shame that Lizzie had to go home and miss tryouts. They came to realize that Lizzie had made an excuse not to tryout. When questioned about it, Lizzie finally admitted that she was afraid she wouldn't make the team and, if she did, that she wouldn't get the questions right at the tournament. Rather than take that risk, Lizzie just decided not to try out for the team.

Trey's teacher used diagnostic pretesting and curriculum compacting, allowing students who already mastered the content, skills, and concepts to work on **independent study projects** rather than "learning" and practicing what they already know. Trey had decided to learn about the rainforest for his independent study. He had several options for products or projects as part of his independent study, and he excitedly told his teacher he wanted to create a learning center and teach a lesson. Trey spent weeks learning all about the rainforest, focusing on the need for conservation and what people could do to help preserve the rainforest. He created activities for a learning center and was going to plan his lesson when he suddenly realized he had never taught his classmates before. They knew he was studying the rainforest, and because he was a soccer star and a good student, they were expecting to learn a lot. They talked about how fun it would be to have him as a teacher. Trey was not sure about his teaching abilities because he had not tried it before. He did not know if he would be good at it, and he was worried he would forget something or not know the answer to something. The day before he was to present his lesson, Trey went to his teacher and explained that he changed his mind and did not want to teach the lesson, even though he had done all of the work and was prepared for it. He did not want to chance letting down the expectations of his classmates.

Kara usually sat outside at recess just watching the other girls doing cartwheels. In P.E., she would get in line at the gymnastics mats when they had centers to choose from. She would watch the other students intently, but then on her turn, she would make an excuse and move to the back of the line or another center. Kara read books about gymnastics and loved to watch it on television. When encouraged to try some gymnastics in P.E., Kara refused, and she would not join the other kids on the playground while they were doing gymnastics. One day at recess, Kara began telling her teacher all about how to do a cartwheel. Next, she started to tell her teacher about how to do flips on the bar. She could explain all of the technical aspects of the gymnastics moves. When her teacher found out Kara had not tried any gymnastics—even though the other kids invited her to play with them, the P.E. teacher had encouraged her, and her parents had offered to sign her up for a gymnastics class—she asked Kara why she would not try to do gymnastics. Kara explained that she knew how to do it, but she did not feel graceful and was not sure her body could do it.

Risk Evaders are afraid to take chances that might expose the fact that they are not perfect. They do not want others or themselves to see their weaknesses or to know that they are not flawless. Sometimes, especially in sports or arts requiring both mind and body, Risk Evaders may be avoiding a task due to asynchronous development, when their mind has developed faster than their body (Miller et al., 2012; Morelock, 1992; Silverman, 1993a, 1993b; Tannenbaum, 1992). Although they see in their mind exactly what they want to do and understand the skills and concepts necessary to achieve it, they are afraid that their body will not perform to their standards. They expect to be perfect the first time they try and every subsequent time. Elena could see the intricate details that a botanist sees in a flower and even could notice the pollen on the stamen, but she feared she could not produce that image with hands that had the dexterity of a 10-year-old. Although Kara could explain all of the procedural knowledge necessary to perform many gymnastics moves and even understood some of the physics behind it, she was afraid that her body could not do what her mind understood it needed to do.

It is not only asynchronous development that may cause Risk Evaders to avoid taking chances. Risk Evaders are one example of how the different descriptions of ways perfectionism is exhibited are not exclusive—for instance, Academic Achievers like Lizzie and Trey also may be Risk Evaders. The primary characteristic of Risk Evaders is that they fear failure to achieve their standards and ideals so they decide not to attempt the task. Children like Jacob might not be faced with asynchronous development or may not exhibit perfectionism in other ways, but they still are afraid that they will not meet their own expectations. They do not delight in the process or in their attempts because they are overly focused on the outcome and the possibility that it will not be perfect. Therefore, they choose not to try rather than undertake the task and possibly not succeed at a level that meets their personal standards. Risk Evaders are paralyzed by their fear, rationalizing that if they never attempt the task, they do not have to risk rejection or criticism from themselves or from others (Adderholdt & Goldberg, 1999).

Strategies for the Classroom

As with other types of perfectionistic behaviors, one of the most potent strategies for helping Risk Evaders avoid unhealthy perfectionistic behaviors and instead focus on positive aspects of motivation and goal setting is for educators to develop a safe classroom environment that encourages risk-taking. Risk Evaders put enough pressure on themselves to be perfect and are afraid to fail without having to fear ridicule from their peers or admonishment from an authority figure. Before they will even consider taking a risk in the classroom, Risk Evaders need to feel supported within the classroom, which requires the entire class to make a commitment to cultivate a safe environment. This environment is essential; otherwise, students fear not just their own rejection of their work as faulty, but also derision from others. To help establish a risk-taking and supportive environment, we suggest some community-building and risk-taking activities in Chapter 9.

Successful Strategies for the Classroom

- Develop a safe classroom environment that encourages risk-taking.
- Encourage students to try new experiences with unknown outcomes.
- Provide smaller opportunities within the classroom to take risks.
- Help students focus on process and revisions rather than on outcomes.
- Help students set future goals based on risk-taking experiences.
- Redefine success as taking a risk.

Risk Evaders need encouragement to try new experiences that may seem challenging and to regard these challenges as adventurous and exciting rather than as daunting. They need to be applauded for their efforts and for tackling something new instead of only being commended on their final products or successes. Without taking a risk, students cannot experience success or the delight of overcoming an obstacle. However, when they do take a risk, they need to know that the risk itself is a success because they will not be flawless or get the outcome they want every time. Helping students move their focus from being perfect to accepting challenges will give them more opportunities for success. Again, this all depends on the classroom being a safe environment for the students to take risks.

> *Risk Evaders need to feel supported within the classroom, which requires the entire class to make a commitment to cultivate a safe environment.*

For some Risk Evaders, especially in the upper elementary grades and later, their identity may be tied to being highly successful. Thus, they may be afraid they will be seen as a fraud or imposter if they take a risk and are not flawless. Furthermore, they may have been avoiding risks for quite some time, only trying something when they are certain they can succeed. As an educator, you can give these students smaller opportunities for risk, although you must be careful not confuse this with opportunities for success. To be a risk, it must be a challenge to the student and the outcome must be uncertain. Although competitions are one type of risky situation that you can expose your students to, some Risk Evaders may not be ready for a statewide or districtwide competition. Instead, the classroom or even a small group of like-ability peers might provide an appropriate situation for risk-taking. You also should remember that not all risk-taking must be competitive situations, like Trey's opportunity to teach his classmates.

Some students may need even smaller opportunities for risk that can be done with minimal exposure to peers. Simply giving a piece of writing or artwork to an educator for feedback is a big step for some students. One strategy to help students set a goal that involves a risk and then attempt it without fear of others knowing they "failed" is to have them set a goal and write it in their classroom journal or on an index card that you collect. Ask them to try something they have been afraid to try or that they have not wanted to risk. Then, have them make a plan for when and how they will try the activity. At the end of a set amount of time, have the students go back to where they wrote down the goal and reflect on the experience. Focus the children's attention on whether or not they took a risk and attempted the activity and what they gained from taking the risk rather than whether they were successful or not. In fact, this is an excellent opportunity to help them redefine "success." If they want to share their goal and the outcome with their classmates, they can and should. Otherwise, they can keep their attempt to themselves and avoid exposing the risk they took.

Risk Evaders, like Aggravated Accuracy Assessors, also need guidance in placing their focus on the process and revisions rather than only on the final outcome. By facing challenges, students can discover both their strengths and weaknesses and set future goals. Setting future goals after a risk-taking event or task sets students up to take a risk at another event or task and to focus on a specific aspect of their performance rather than only on being perfect. This also redefines success so that it is not a global evaluation of the child's performance or product compared to their ideal. Rather, the definition of success can be an evaluation of how they have progressed toward meeting their goals and whether they took a chance and tried.

Strategies for the Home

One way that you, as a caregiver, can help Risk Evaders is to engage in family activities. These activities should include things that all members enjoy, not things that one family member with special talent will dominate in. Participation in these types of activities can help children realize the fun of participating in activities that provide enjoyment without being skilled in them. Some example activities might include a community or church choir, softball league, or even informal activities, such as badminton in the backyard. Some families host karaoke nights, croquet events, or even Twister tournaments. The key is to have fun and take humor in less-than-perfect performances. Encouraging the entire family to try entirely new activities, such as whitewater rafting on vacation or dining at a new restaurant that offers unique cuisine, also can show the importance of risk-taking.

Successful Strategies for the Home

- Adopt activities that are fun but not an area of strength.
- Emphasize enjoyment over perfection.
- Upon completion of projects, notice areas of strength and improvement.
- Share joy upon completion of projects.
- Encourage intellectual risk-taking.

In all activities, enjoyment should be the focus, rather than perfection. This applies to informal, extracurricular, and academic tasks. As a caregiver, you can help to emphasize process over product. In this way, you can help children realize the joy that comes from doing activities, rather than the frustration that comes from an emphasis on unrealistic standards.

When your child is working on a big project or assignment, you can help by taking a moment to reflect with your child when the assignment is completed. This should be done before the teacher has assessed the project. You can help your child notice their areas of strength in the product and also find areas for improvement. This also can be a time for celebration with your child. The key is to help your child increase **intrinsic** or **internal motivation** for completion of projects, rather than relying on the external motivation of grades and evaluations. You can help your child realize the joy that occurs when a project is completed.

This joy also can be modeled by you as a caregiver. When you finish a large project at work or around the house, you also can host a celebration for the family to share in the joy. These types of celebrations—even if they are as simple as ordering pizza, renting a movie at home, or allowing the person who took the risk to choose dinner or the family game—can provide opportunities for you and your children to discuss the joys of taking intellectual risks and finishing projects.

> *As a caregiver, you can help to emphasize process over product.*

Finally, you can do much for your children by encouraging them to enter contests and take intellectual risks. Intellectual risks can be simple for caregivers to incorporate into everyday activities. For example, when selecting books, adults can encourage children to select a book a bit longer or at a slightly more advanced level than usual. As children are challenged by this, adults can read with their children to support their learning. Other ideas might be to watch a foreign movie with subtitles, enter a local poetry contest, or try a challenging crossword puzzle together.

You can emphasize the benefits of trying things in which you probably will not be the winner, such as gaining experience and networking with others. Additionally, you can discuss with your children times when you took a risk. These types of examples could include job searches or college applications. Be sure to include times when the goal was obtained as well as times when you were not necessarily successful. The lessons learned and benefits for this approach should be emphasized.

Final Thoughts

Risk Evaders are reluctant to try new activities or take a chance on something in which they might not be successful. This can occur in athletic, artistic, or academic domains. Sometimes, educators and families might perceive Risk Evaders as being lazy, as they often will choose an activity in which they are confident they will succeed (usually an easier task) rather than one in which they will have to work hard to do well.

However, it is these children's fear of failure and of not being perfect that is preventing them from trying more challenging activities. Educators and families can help Risk Evaders by developing safe environments for them to take risks and by encouraging a focus on the process rather than the final outcome. They should applaud children for their efforts and for trying new, challenging activities.

CHAPTER 6

The Controlling Image Manager

"I Could Have if I Wanted to"

Craig was somewhat athletic and loved to run and play with his friends on the playground. Recently, the majority of Craig's class has played tag during recess. They set up boundaries that everyone had to stay within so that the arena was not too large for the size of the group. If someone stepped outside the boundaries, they automatically were "It." Craig loved to taunt whoever was It, especially when it was one of his good friends. He would run near them and yell, "You can't catch me!" However, as soon as the person who was It ran close to him, Craig would jump out of bounds, automatically making him It, declaring, "I wanted to be It!" This would, understandably, frustrate his classmates and friends.

Rachelle was a mathematically talented fourth grader with extremely strong number sense. She was very excited when her teacher announced they would be holding a classroom tournament for Rachelle's favorite math game. Rachelle loved to play the game, and any time they had free time in the classroom she would play with her classmates or even by herself if no one else would play. When the day of the classroom tournament came, Rachelle was very focused, her skills were evident, and she easily won. Then, Rachelle competed in the schoolwide tournament, where she played the winners from the other five fourth-grade classes and all six fifth-grade classes. Rachelle again won easily against the other fourth graders and most fifth graders. In the final round, Rachelle finally was challenged somewhat, but she still won by a significant margin. Next for Rachelle was the district tournament, where the winners from all 23 elementary schools would compete. Although Rachelle was confident in her math skills, loved the game, and had been extremely successful in the classroom and school-wide tournaments, Rachelle's teacher overhead her telling her friends that she planned to intentionally get enough penalties to disqualify her from the district tournament. When her teacher asked her about her plan, Rachelle explained that she really could win if she wanted to, but she didn't want to that much. After further prompting, Rachelle admitted that math was her "thing" and she felt like she had to win but that she was not sure what her competition would be like.

Usually on report card day, Karl came home and immediately showed his mom his report card. He was an academically talented student who took pride in his grades. Plus, he knew that the local bowling alley offered two free games for every A and one free game for every B, so he loved getting to take his report card there on report card day. Karl's mom knew it was report card day, and Karl's older brother had already given his to his mom to look at and sign. However, dinner had come and gone, and Karl still had not shown his mom his report card. She asked the boys if they were ready to go to the bowling alley, and Karl reluctantly went to get ready. Karl's mom followed him up to his room so they could talk alone, and she asked him if she could see his report card. With a great big sigh, Karl walked over to his backpack, got out his binder, and started rummaging for his report card. Before he handed it to his mom, without looking up from his binder, he said to her, "You know, I could have gotten all A's if I wanted to. I didn't really want to this time." When she looked at Karl's report card, his mother noticed that he had earned a B+ in social studies. She asked Karl if it had been a difficult topic this marking period, and he responded, "Nah. It was just economics, but I didn't really want to get all A's. Maybe I will next time."

Latisha had been practicing and practicing her jump rope skills. No matter what her friends were playing at recess, Latisha was on the blacktop jumping rope. Sometimes she would jump rope with other children, and other times she would grab a single rope to work on individual tricks. She had mastered many of the stunts she had seen the school's jump rope team do during their school performances. Latisha especially loved when her class was out at recess at the same time as the fourth and fifth graders because she had made a couple of friends who were on the jump rope team, and they would show her new tricks to work on. In January, the P.E. teacher held tryouts for the jump rope team, which was the first opportunity for third graders like Latisha to try out. However, Latisha decided not to go to the tryouts. The next week, when the newest members of the jump rope team were announced on the morning announcements, Latisha explained aloud that she would have made the team if she had wanted to, but she would rather just jump rope at recess instead of on a team.

Every year the Parent Teacher Organization (PTO) held an artistic competition for the elementary school students. The students submitted creative expressions, in the form of poetry, photography, collages, drawing, or music, on the annual theme, which was "heroes" this year. Mark was very excited about the competition because he had been wanting to share some of his photography. Last year, when he was in third grade, his uncle had bought him a high-tech digital camera that he had learned to use on manual mode. Mark loved his camera, and he read photography books to learn different ways of using the camera and to learn about composition. As soon as the theme for the competition was announced, Mark began thinking about what he would photograph for his submission, and he began taking even more photos than usual. When his teacher collected the submissions on the day they were due, she overheard Mark explaining to his friends that he didn't really want to win—that a "real" photographer does not need recognition, and he did not submit his best photo.

Controlling Image Managers not only expect themselves to be perfect, but also want others to regard them as being perfect. They do not want others to see their flaws or detect any imperfections. If they are afraid they cannot meet their own expectations or the expectations of others, they may choose to eliminate themselves from activities intentionally to prevent failure. Rather than just choosing not to participate, as Risk Evaders will do, Controlling Image Managers set up the situation so that they can think, and say, that they *could have* succeeded and *could have* been perfect if they had *tried* or *wanted* to be successful.

Controlling Image Managers often exhibit other types of perfectionistic behaviors as well. First and foremost, they often avoid risks while managing their image. Although some Controlling Image Managers, like Mark, will attempt the task but set themselves up with an explanation in the event that they do not meet expectations, other Controlling Image Managers, like Rachelle and Latisha, will avoid the task while giving an explanation that preserves their image. Controlling Image Managers like Karl also might be Academic Achievers. These children might have their identity so tightly connected to being academically "perfect" that they must try to control their image and identity if they exhibit anything less than academic perfection.

One problem often faced by Controlling Image Managers is that the other children they are around, such as those in their class or neighborhood, may get frustrated with them because they always must win or they give up. For instance, the other children playing tag with Craig never had a chance to tag him fairly. Other children may resent that Controlling Image Managers rarely participate fully in competitive situations and only do so when they absolutely are certain they will win.

> *Controlling Image Managers expect themselves to be perfect and want others to see them as being perfect. Therefore, they set up situations so that they have no perceived flaws and their image as perfect is not tarnished.*

Strategies for the Classroom

One of the important issues that must be addressed in the classroom is the frustration that other children in the class may feel because they never have a fair chance to win in a competitive situation with Controlling Image Managers. This might create tension during recess, review games in the class, and other competitive situations. One strategy to help is to conduct some small-group role-playing, which may help Controlling Image Managers better understand others' feelings in competitive situations. Not only do they need help to understand the frustration of their peers, but also they must realize that they are not expected to be perfect or to win whenever competing against others. Controlling Image Managers benefit from reading and discussing the losses of their role models in competitive situations. The losses might be from athletes, chess players, artists, or any other competitor, as long as they illustrate that those who chose to compete do not always win yet are still highly regarded. Inviting guest speakers into the class to discuss their personal defeats, particularly in competitive situations, would make the idea more realistic and personal to students. Students might relate to these individuals and ask these role models questions that help them come to understand the need for personal improvement and not just perfection and winning.

The two of us both find the American Ninja Warrior competition to be useful for such discussions with children. Clips of this show are easily found on YouTube, and there are examples of both personal athletic competition and team competition, as well as adult and junior competition.

The athletic performances (both successes and failures) provide opportunities for discussion, as do the back stories that are shared about what the athletes have overcome to get where they are, including multiple failures for some. The ability of the athletes to continue after not completing the course, and the sense of community between the competitors, makes this show an excellent example of how a family can incorporate lessons about perfectionism into family time.

Successful Strategies for the Classroom

- Address frustrations from classmates through role-playing.
- Read about and discuss role models' losses or failures and invite guest speakers to share their experiences.
- Help students set personal goals, not comparative goals.
- Encourage risk-taking.
- Applaud student attempts and willingness to compete.

Unfortunately, Controlling Image Managers do not take pleasure in competition and in trying their hardest. Instead, they focus excessively on winning and on being the best. They expect to be perfect, including being better than their classmates and friends. Controlling Image Managers need help setting personal goals that focus on their own performance prior to a competitive event, rather than focusing on how they do relative to others. This will allow them to strive for a standard that is based on their personal performance instead of relying on others being "less perfect" than them. By setting personal goals focused on their own performance, Controlling Image Managers are encouraged to compete and improve, regardless of their competition. This strategy helped Rachelle immensely. When her teacher heard her plan to intentionally eliminate herself from the district tournament, she talked with Rachelle about her personal goals for the tournament. Having personal goals that did not focus on the other students competing helped Rachelle decide to take the game home to practice and improve rather than committing to her original plan.

Like Risk Evaders, Controlling Image Managers need encouragement to try challenging, competitive situations and situations in which they are not sure they will succeed or be flawless. Again, applauding these students for their efforts and for attempting the task is essential, rather than just commending them on their final successes. Controlling Image Managers cannot truly enjoy their success or understand the feeling of accomplishment when overcoming an obstacle or winning a competitive situation unless they allow themselves to risk not being the best or being perfect. They must experience (and come to understand) that they will not always be perfect or win but they do not have to make excuses for their performance. They need to know that they are not expected to be flawless, to be better than others, or to never show a fault, but that they are just expected to try and to work on personal improvement.

Strategies for the Home

The Controlling Image Manager can pose particular problems for families. It can be frustrating to deal with these behaviors at home and even more difficult to help these children negotiate friendships and peer relationships. It is heartbreaking to see children lose friendships due to their own behaviors, even when family members find the same behaviors annoying.

Successful Strategies for the Home

- Hold discussions during noncompetitive times.
- Role-play competitive situations.
- Play semicompetitive games at home.
- Carefully monitor competitive situations with peers or siblings and provide support.
- Find examples of competitions in media and discuss them.
- Help your child set personal goals rather than comparative goals.

The first step to help address this problem might be to have conversations with Controlling Image Managers during times in which they are not involved in a contest or game. When away from the controlling situation, they may be able to talk more rationally about their behavior. Additionally, it may be helpful to introduce the topic by telling the story of a similar child who does not play by the rules. This may help to defuse the situation further and allow for a deeper discussion in which your child feels less defensive. At the conclusion of the story, you then may wish to apply the lessons learned to your child's own life.

Another strategy that might be helpful is to role-play competitive situations at home. For example, you may ask your child to pretend that they are losing a game of checkers. Then your child could have the opportunity to react. This could be tailored to your child's interests and areas of trouble when interacting with peers. Appropriate reactions to similar situations could be the topic of a family discussion or of a conversation between you and your child. Alternatively, you could act out inappropriate reactions or play the role of your child. This may help your child to understand how their reactions may be frustrating to others. This type of activity should be followed with a conversation about alternative reactions that would have better outcomes. Some children might find it less threatening to talk about how someone else should react. For instance, when watching a television show or movie, or reading a book, in which a character is losing a game, talk with your child about the different ways the character could react and how their reactions would affect others. You might even ask your child how they would react if the character behaved in certain ways and they were friends. This might allow the child to see how certain behaviors are perceived by others without becoming defensive and feeling flawed.

Playing more competitive games at home also may provide opportunities to help children cope with not winning all of the time. During games, whether they are sports, board games, or video games, you, as the caregiver, should model appropriate behavior. You also can role model good sportsmanship in accepting your wins and losses when playing games as a family. In addition, you should not allow your child to give up or get out of the situation when faced with a challenge or allow your child to succeed each time to avoid confrontation. This additional practice in authentic situations may help your child cope with their own imperfections. Family game time provides children with a safe environment in which to fail.

You also have the opportunity to observe many of your child's competitive situations when they are interacting with peers. Formal events, such as soccer games or spelling bees, as well as informal events, such as play-dates, provide situations in which you can carefully monitor your child's interactions with peers and their response to competition. Prior to beginning such activities, you should plan ahead with your child to develop healthy strategies to cope with loss or even the potential for loss. These conversations can focus on helping your child set personal goals based on their own achievements rather than on comparing their performance to others. For example, the goal for a soccer game might not be to score more goals than a teammate or even to win the game. Instead, a personal goal might be to pass the soccer ball to more team members than last week. With informal events, like a playdate to play board games or an outdoor game, you should talk with your child about focusing on simply having fun and enjoying the company of their friends rather than on always winning. You also should be aware of when your child might be exhibiting behaviors to avoid the appearance of lack of success. When these situations arise, you can be available to discuss the matter privately with your child. Finding a discreet way to make your child aware of the situation and their behavior may help your child to avoid such problems in the future.

Finally, it often is helpful for families to find examples of people who have lost competitions. Examples can be found in sporting events, game shows, and even reality television shows. When a favorite team loses a game, you can emphasize that the team is still made of excellent athletes even if they lost a game. You can discuss what the team did well that day and also ask your child what the team should work on at practice before the next game. You can look at examples of Olympic athletes who did not win the gold medal but were overjoyed to win another medal when such victory was unexpected. You can model respect for losing contestants on game shows by discussing the merits and behaviors of the players after the results are announced. The individual performance of the participants should be emphasized rather than their relative strength compared to other players.

Final Thoughts

Controlling Image Managers are especially focused on how others perceive them. They tend to set up situations so that they can think and also tell others that they *could* have succeeded if they had tried, as Craig did in the game of tag. For them, perfection is a strong part of their identity, and they are afraid to have others see any flaws in them. Educators and families of Controlling Image Managers can help by encouraging risk-taking and attempts to compete. Role-playing situations also may help these children, especially if their peers are frustrated with their behavior.

CHAPTER 7

The Procrastinating Perfectionist

"If It Stays in My Mind, Then I Can't Fail"

As the date for state testing neared, Elliott's teacher announced a social studies review project. The students were to create a social studies review board game over a period of several weeks. After they discussed the requirements for the project, the students went to lunch, where Elliott sat with a clipboard and began planning his game. At recess that day, Elliott excitedly shared with his teacher his intricate vision. He already had a mental picture of the board and had begun to work out the rules.

Whenever his teacher or a classmate mentioned the project, Elliott got very excited and talked about his game. However, just days before the project was due, Elliott's dad asked him how the project was coming. Elliott admitted that he had not yet started on the project. Moreover, besides the plan in his head and the few sketches from that first day at lunch, Elliott did not have a plan to create his game. After a lecture from his dad, Elliott promised to work on his game, but the night before it was due, he still had not started and was not sure what to do.

Ms. Peters announced to her class that they would be competing in a national vocabulary contest. Victor was extremely excited and announced right then that he would earn a perfect score. The contest was made up of five vocabulary assessments, and students were given the vocabulary list to study prior to each assessment date. The day before the first assessment, Victor admitted to Ms. Peters that he had not yet begun studying. That night, he stayed up late studying. After he finished the contest the next day, he announced, "I didn't have enough time to study, so I couldn't get them all right."

Every night Olivia's parents struggled with her to complete her homework. She would come home from school, go to her desk, and get out her books, but by dinner she had made no progress on her homework. After dinner, she would return to her desk, but by bedtime, she still was sitting there and would break into tears because she had not completed her homework. Olivia's parents made an appointment to meet with her teacher, confused about why a young child would have so much homework. Olivia's teacher explained that the homework should only take Olivia about 30 minutes and asked about her work habits. Confused, Olivia's parents explained that she had a desk dedicated to her homework in a quiet location in the house with no television. She would sit at the desk with her homework for hours, explaining that she understood everything, but still would not complete the work by bedtime. That evening, Olivia's mom sat with her while she started on her homework. She soon realized that Olivia would sit for lengths of time staring at the paper without doing any work. She was not daydreaming or doing something else, but she just was not writing answers on the paper. When she asked Olivia what she was doing, Olivia explained that she was afraid she would write the wrong answers and would work on those problems later, and then she started looking at some other problems. This went on for the next hour, with Olivia not committing to writing any answers although she looked at every problem. When her mom asked her to tell her what she thought the answers might be, Olivia answered the majority of them correctly.

Krystal, who loved science, was very excited when her teacher passed out information about the local university's summer enrichment program. She could not believe they had a chemistry class for elementary students! Enrollment in the program was limited and thus competitive, so students were required to write an essay on why they wanted to be in the class, their parents had to complete an application form and send in a copy of the student's report card, and their teachers had to complete a recommendation form. Krystal gave the form for the recommendation to her teacher the day after she took the information home and obtained her parents' approval, and her dad copied her report card and completed the application. However, on the postmark date, Krystal still had not even begun her essay. When her dad asked her if she still wanted to go, Krystal started crying and said she wanted to go more than anything. Then when he asked her why she had not written the essay, she explained that she knew what she wanted to say but was afraid she could not write it well enough to get in. Because the deadline was fast approaching, she sat down and wrote her essay in less than 15 minutes and gave it to her dad to mail with her application.

Ryan's parents were tired of fighting with him to complete long-term projects. Every time one was assigned, they ended up helping him the night or two nights before it was due. He always had a grand vision in his mind for how to complete the project, but he never seemed to work on it before the due date was imminent. They were hoping that because Ryan now was in the fifth grade, he might have matured some and learned from the stress of his previous projects. However, they found out with the first assigned project that Ryan still procrastinated when assigned a project and then panicked at the last minute. They were not sure what to do to help him. It seemed that they could not find a way to motivate him to start his project sooner.

Procrastinating Perfectionists have a perfect vision in their mind, a perfect outcome that they expect to reach, and very high standards for themselves and their products, but they fear that they are not able to achieve that vision. This fear paralyzes them from taking action, leading to procrastination. Unlike Risk Evaders, who intentionally do not attempt the task so that they will not fail, and unlike Controlling Image Managers, who make excuses and save face, Procrastinating Perfectionists have every intention of completing the task but just seem to wait until the last minute to try to accomplish it. In the back of their minds, Procrastinating Perfectionists may have thoughts that lead to inaction, such as, "If I never complete the project, I don't have to risk getting a bad grade" (Adderholdt & Goldberg, 1999), or even, "If I never complete the project, I don't have to be frustrated that the final project did not turn out the way I wanted it to or did not meet my standards."

One common incidence of procrastination for these students is long-term projects assigned at school, like those with which Elliott and Ryan struggled. When assigned a substantial project, some children, particularly gifted children, will plan elaborate and creative projects. They can see the details in their mind and become extremely enthusiastic about the project. They might share their ideas with their peers, educators, and caregivers, but they are not as excited to get started on the project itself. Although they may continue to think about what they envision the final product to be like, they fear that it will not turn out the way they imagined it or are intimidated by the formidable tasks ahead. They want to do the project, but they just cannot get started on it and put it off as long as possible, until they essentially have no way of completing the project to their standards due to time constraints. Often, this leads to frustration and disappointment on their part.

Some Procrastinating Perfectionists, like Victor and Krystal, are paralyzed in a competitive situation by their fear of failure and not meeting their standards and their mind's ideal. Then, they use their procrastination as a way to control their image, to say to themselves or others that they could have done better if they had started sooner or had had more time, regardless of how much time they actually were given. Procrastinating Perfectionists typically have a vision of perfection in their mind, but their anxiety about not achieving it leads to procrastination, which then allows them to preserve their egos by giving them an "excuse" for not being perfect or achieving their standards.

For many families, the continued pattern of procrastination from Procrastinating Perfectionists can be quite frustrating. They begin to feel that they constantly are nagging their children to get their schoolwork and other projects completed. Although their children might do high-quality work, particularly if they are Academic Achievers as well, it is a constant struggle to get them to sit down and commit to completing work on the task until just before it is due. Worse, if the child also is an Aggravated Accuracy Assessor, the combination of waiting until the last minute to begin and then fixating on every detail may cause the child, and consequently their families, extreme frustration, anxiety, and distress.

Strategies for the Classroom

Procrastinating Perfectionists have a tendency to look at a project or task as a whole and to become overwhelmed with their vision and their fear that they cannot accomplish it perfectly. These children need help breaking down large tasks into smaller subtasks with concrete deadlines to help motivate them to complete parts prior to the main deadline. Educators who work with Procrastinating Perfectionists need to recognize their need for assistance and that they do have a vision but may not understand the steps necessary to commence work on the project and make the vision a reality. Students need to have ownership of their work, especially so that they can use their motivation in a healthy and beneficial manner in the future rather than continuing to be paralyzed by their perfectionistic tendencies. Therefore, you should not provide them a preplanned set of smaller tasks, goals, and deadlines. Rather, you should work with students together to create a plan, breaking the larger task into smaller segments and setting goals along the way (see the example on the following pages). It is important for you to allow Procrastinating Perfectionists to continue to hold high standards and expectations for the final product. But by breaking projects into smaller tasks and goals, Procrastinating Perfectionists now have a process to focus on and standards to meet along the way so that they do not become so overwhelmed and afraid that they cannot meet their standards. Figure 6 shows how a project might be broken down into parts. Furthermore, this helps Procrastinating Perfectionists shift their focus from the final product to the process and from the outcome to the effort that goes into the process. This will help them use their perfectionism in a healthy way and overcome their paralyzing fear.

Successful Strategies for the Classroom

- Help students break large projects into smaller subtasks.
- Help students create a schedule with buffers.
- Help students recognize the need to prioritize and not overextend.
- Focus on process and effort rather than on outcomes and final products.
- Celebrate success throughout the learning process, not just at the final deadline or culminating event.

When helping Procrastinating Perfectionists create subtasks and goals, you also need to help them learn how to develop schedules. These children, in particular, need a schedule with **buffers** built into them so that when something does not go as planned or does not meet their expectations and standards, they do not feel that they have failed already and that there is no need to continue. Being able to work toward their standards and goals still is important for these students, and experiencing success along the way will help them avoid becoming anxious and overwhelmed with fear of failure.

In addition to creating subtasks, goals, and schedules, Procrastinating Perfectionists need help prioritizing. Children who are **overextended** with afterschool activities or who are Academic Achievers who want to be perfect in all subjects may be more prone to feeling overwhelmed and become paralyzed with fear that they cannot be perfect in all of their endeavors at the same time. These children need help examining their schedule to iden-

FIGURE 6
Sample Task Broken Down

Social Studies Review Game

Assigned: March 16
Due Date: April 21

Assignment: Create a review game for 2–4 players. Provide all of the necessary components (board, moving pieces, question cards, answers, rules, etc.). See your assignment sheet for the full description and for the scoring rubric. Be sure to refer to both of those documents when creating your game.

Tasks to be completed:

* **Outline your game.** Decide the objective (how to win), what the board should be like (you can design it like other games you have played), what happens when you get a question right or wrong, and how players will move on the board (if that is part of your game). Suggested due date: March 20.

* **Create a plan.** Once you have outlined your game, you will know what you need for a finished game. Look at the tasks below and your outline and also ask a parent to sit down with you and look at your family's calendar. Decide when you want to finish each piece (see the suggested dates below). Due date: March 24.

* **Write questions and answers.** Remember that you have to meet the requirements on the assignment sheet, with a certain number of questions per topic. When you write the questions, go ahead and record the answers. Suggestion: Complete 3–5 questions per day. Due date: Have your questions written by April 14. Remember that Spring Break is April 4–13, so you might want to do extra at the beginning so you don't have to do as many during Spring Break!

* **Revise cards.** On April 14, we will have a session to read each other's questions and make suggestions. Suggested completion date: Have your cards revised by April 17 so your family has time to play your game and you can make further revisions, if needed, before the final due date.

FIGURE 6, continued

- **Create your board.** Your board will have to match your outline. Think about special squares, how to win, when players will answer questions, etc. This is your chance to be creative, but remember that you have a time limit and most of your points will come from the questions, not from the board design. Suggested date: If you have plans for Spring Break, finish this by April 3. If you will be home for Spring Break and want to work on it then, plan to have it finished by April 14.
- **Write your rules.** Write your rules, making sure you include everything necessary (see the assignment sheet). Be sure to ask a family member to read your rules to see if they understand. Suggested date: Have these completed by April 17. Then have your family or friends play the game. Ask them to read the rules and play while you watch. That way you can see if you forgot to write a rule, did not write a rule clearly, or need to make any other changes.
- **Gather or create other necessary materials.** Don't forget about any materials you need, such as moving pieces, dice, etc. Suggested date: Gather these by April 17 so your family or friends can play.

Note. Notice the suggestion for doing a little each day (writing questions) and creating an outline/plan using the suggestions and task list as well as the family calendar.

tify when other tests and projects are due or when they have an important extracurricular event and then determine what is most important to them. If they have an elaborate project plan or challenging goal in mind, they may need help recognizing that they might not be able to put as much effort and focus into other tasks as usual. This will help them understand that they cannot be perfect and meet their high standards in all things at all times. Procrastinating Perfectionists, particularly if they are Academic Achievers or Aggravated Accuracy Assessors, need help recognizing that something has to give and that they do have limitations to what they can accomplish, especially under deadlines. Although it is important to have high standards, to set goals, and to create subtasks, these children also need to prioritize and recognize their limits. Again, you need to help these children understand that their high standards are valid and that they can excel, but also realize and acknowledge that they cannot be flawless or "the best" at everything. They may need help to see that when they have too much to accomplish, rather than feeling overwhelmed and becoming paralyzed with fear because they cannot meet their standards, they sometimes must adjust their expectations and sacrifice a little of one thing to excel at something else. When working with Procrastinating Perfectionists to create subtasks, goals, and a schedule, you must help them examine the entire picture and what currently requires their attention rather than just focusing on the assigned task.

For the Procrastinating Perfectionists who use their procrastination as a way to save face and control their image, addressing their fear of failure and their tendency to procrastinate will help alleviate the ego-saving behavior that they use along with procrastination. Additionally, the focus on process and effort rather than on outcomes and evaluation of the final product will help them be able to identify strengths and weaknesses rather than directing their attention toward an absolute definition of success and failure. By doing so, their identity will not be tied entirely to the outcome, so they will not need to make excuses. Rather, they can take pride in their efforts and in the process, experiencing success at what they have done along the way, including completing subtasks and meeting midpoint goals.

Strategies for the Home

Families who have experienced the "**last-minute meltdown**" when a child has not begun, much less finished, a major project the night before the due date know the difficulty that Procrastinating Perfectionists can pose to families. In the moment when the child is approaching (or experiencing) a breakdown, the important task for you is to help your child find a way to defuse the situation and relax their personal standards for the project. The goal at the last minute is to finish the project while maintaining healthy sleeping habits for your child. This might mean that your child does not have the opportunity to implement all of their ideas, but you can help your child recognize their own limitations given the amount of time available. Alternatively, if your child cannot finish on their own (without the family helping to do the work) within the remaining time while getting adequate sleep, the goal might be to help your child accept consequences for a late project. You must be sure your child knows this is not a "free pass" or another opportunity to procrastinate. You can do this by working with your child right then to create a work plan for how to accomplish the project not to perfection, but to the degree it can be turned in as close to the original due date as possible. Be sure to have your child sign this as a contract with you, and hold your child to it, whether the teacher will accept late work or not.

Most importantly, you, as a caregiver, must work with your child to prevent these situations from happening in the first place. When projects, contests, and opportunities are announced, you have the opportunity to work with your child to develop a plan to complete the objectives. These plans should set dates for specific goals and allow time for "redos," rough drafts, and revising. After the plan is in place, you should regularly check in with your child to help them complete their goals. This may need to be done daily in the beginning but may become less frequent as your child develops independence in working toward their goals. The blank project planner in Figure 7 and sample calendar in Figure 8 can help caregivers and children work together to set reasonable goals for upcoming projects.

Successful Strategies for the Home

- Help your child find ways to relax their standards during crunch time.
- Help your child make a plan for finishing long-term assignments.
- Check in regularly with your child to help maintain good work habits.
- Find nonstressful times to discuss time management with your child.
- Communicate regularly with your child's educators.
- Use family projects as a way to model positive behaviors.

Sometimes it may become apparent that your child does not always convey information to you about upcoming projects and activities. In this case, it is imperative that you have quality communication with your child's educators. This communication can provide information about upcoming events as well as provide feedback about your child's progress. Truly, when families and educators work together, children ultimately benefit. Although

FIGURE 7
Blank Project Planner

Project Name _____

Time Period _____ Due Date _____

Tasks   1.
               2.
               3.
               4.
               5.
               6.
               7.
               8.

email and class websites make this direct communication with your child's teacher easy, do not take all responsibility off your child. Help your child see the importance of communicating with you and their educators, and be sure to ask your child if there are any upcoming projects or tests. If your child's school or teacher does not have students use an agenda or planner to write down homework, projects, and tests, you might purchase one or provide a small notebook where your child can write down what they have coming up and can share with you each night.

> *When families and educators work together, children ultimately benefit.*

The best time to talk with children about procrastination is not when they are in the middle of a deadline crisis. Instead, you should find non-stressful times to address these issues with your child. The consequences of postponing projects and procrastination can be discussed. In addition, you can help alleviate your child's unrealistic expectations of their performance on projects and help your child recognize their own limitations in completing projects. You should emphasize to your child that all situations pose limitations for performance and that perfection is never obtainable. Providing an example of a situation in which you had to complete a project

FIGURE 8
Sample Project Calendar

	Week 1	Week 2	Week 3	Week 4
Monday	Pick a state	Finish note-taking	Begin "sloppy copy"	Write final copy
Tuesday	Look online for resources	Organize notes	Work on "sloppy copy"	Finish final copy
Wednesday	Go to library for resources	Write outline	Finish "sloppy copy"	Design poster
Thursday	Begin writing notes	Organize bibliography	*Free day*	Make illustrations
Friday	*Free day*	*Free day*	*Free day*	*Free day*
Saturday	Continue writing notes	Finish up outline	*Free day*	Put together poster
Sunday	Continue writing notes	Finish up outline	Finish "sloppy copy"	Put together poster

to the best of your ability under a deadline might help them see that in the real world, perfection is not always necessary or even ideal.

Finally, families can work together to complete large-scale projects in the home, which gives an outlet for working together in a relaxed environment rather than experiencing the stress of a last-minute school project. Projects might include home improvement, such as building a deck or painting the living room; service projects, such as making a quilt for a homeless shelter or collecting cans for a soup kitchen; craft projects for gifts or decorations; or playing on an informal athletic team. Children, as well as caregivers, should be involved in an active role in these projects. This provides opportunities for caregivers to model appropriate behaviors. It also can give caregivers and children time to discuss the problems that are associated with perfectionism in this context. Additionally, these projects provide teachable moments for families to share. For example, as the adult, you may wish to point out compromises that are made during the process, such as minor imperfections in the home improvement process or less elaborate plans in the service project. You should emphasize the limitations of your own skill, time available, or other circumstances that prevented you from achieving perfection in the task. Then, you could make explicit connections to projects that your child is undergoing at a similar time. Through this process, you and your children can experience the challenges, as well as the rewards, of completing a large-scale project without procrastination.

Final Thoughts

Procrastinating Perfectionists often have grand visions for projects and final products, but they delay working on those projects until there is not enough time to finish them. This often stems from a fear of creating a less-than-perfect product or performing at less than their ideal. Some Procrastinating Perfectionists use their procrastination as a way to control their image, some use it as a way to avoid taking a risk with a new idea, and others simply cannot get past the fear that they will not be able to do as well as they envision. Educators and families can help Procrastinating Perfectionists by guiding them in setting realistic goals leading up to major projects and increasing communication between home and school. They must help Procrastinating Perfectionists with planning their time, creating goals and subtasks, and accepting responsibility.

CHAPTER 8

Identifying Healthy Motivation and Goals and Unhealthy Perfectionism

There is no magic formula that will tell you if your child or student is a perfectionist and whether they have healthy, appropriate motivation and goals or have unhealthy perfectionistic tendencies. The truth of the matter is that many children exhibit perfectionism in some contexts but not in all situations or environments and that they exhibit it to varying degrees. In fact, some families and educators find that when they meet to discuss an issue about a child's unhealthy perfectionistic behaviors, the behaviors are only being exhibited in the home or at school but not both. Similarly, a child may have perfectionistic tendencies only in sports or the arts but not in academics, or even in one subject but not all academic subjects. Children do not consistently exhibit their perfectionistic tendencies. They also may sometimes exhibit positive, **healthy motivation** and goals, and at other times exhibit unhealthy perfectionistic behaviors in the same subject or task. Depending on the context, they may exhibit perfectionism in a different way, and this is affected by many factors, including:

- if they have too many commitments and are spread too thin;
- if they are in a new situation, such as a self-contained gifted and talented program, or being challenged in ways they have not before;
- if they are under particular stress to succeed; or
- if they have not been getting enough sleep.

> Children exhibit perfectionism differently in different contexts. In fact, educators and families may not see the same behaviors in a child.

The Five Types of Perfectionism

The five types of perfectionism are generalizations from what we have observed in children as teachers and parents. Table 5 reviews the five types of perfectionists as noted in the previous chapters. These types are not exclusive categories. That is, a child may exhibit behaviors of more than one type of perfectionism. Furthermore, no child is a particular type all of the time and in all contexts. Table 5 provides a general list of behaviors that describe each type of perfectionism. These are based on our observations and are not a definitive list. Additionally, there is no set number of characteristics that do or do not define each type. That is, you should not calculate a "score" for each type to determine if a particular child could be described as that type of perfectionist or not. Instead, we hope this table will help you identify particular behaviors the child exhibits to help you find possible strategies for helping the child use their perfectionism in a healthy way.

> The focus should not be on labeling a child as a certain type of perfectionist but on finding appropriate strategies to help the child use perfectionism in a healthy way.

TABLE 5

A Summary of the Characteristics of the Five Types of Perfectionists

Type of Perfectionist	Behaviors
Academic Achievers	<ul><li>Identity is tied to academic achievements and performance</li><li>Overly focused on grades</li><li>Concerned with earning less than 100%, considering missing a problem or earning an A- "failure"</li><li>Fixate on extra credit for the sake of earning the points</li><li>Focus on mistakes, which are viewed as a sign of failure and a flaw in identity</li><li>Put forth extreme effort and agonize over turning in perfect work</li><li>Struggle to do homework, which is viewed as an evaluation of intelligence</li><li>Expect mastery on first exposure</li></ul>
Aggravated Accuracy Assessors	<ul><li>Goals are focused on precision and flawless work</li><li>Focus completely on end product and not process</li><li>Deviations from their plan or the "rules" result in frantic "repairing" or "redos"</li><li>Become aggravated at themselves for not doing things exactly "right"</li><li>May be experiencing asynchronous development</li><li>Constantly evaluate projects and become frustrated with their work</li><li>Repeatedly redo work</li><li>Hide work from others</li></ul>

TABLE 5, continued

Type of Perfectionist	Behaviors
Risk Evaders	• Are afraid of taking a chance or trying something challenging because it will expose their imperfections • Hide weaknesses and flaws • Fear of failure results in inaction and avoiding particular tasks • Overly focused on outcomes and the possibility of imperfection • May be experiencing asynchronous development
Controlling Image Managers	• Want others to perceive them as perfect • Focus on avoiding others' detection of their flaws and imperfections • Eliminate themselves from competitive situations rather than not succeeding as a way to avoid the risk • Manage image by saying they "could have" succeeded if they would have attempted the task • Control image because being perfect is tied to identity • May be resented by peers for not competing in a "fair" way
Procrastinating Perfectionists	• Fear inability to achieve vision of perfection, paralyzing them from action • Have intentions to start but never do, or put off projects until the last minute • Become frustrated or disappointed that when they finally start, the time is limited, and their ideal cannot be reached • Sometimes control image by explaining their imperfections as a lack of time for preparation or completion • May do high-quality work but struggle to commit to working on the task and beginning the work

Signs of Unhealthy Perfectionism

Used in a healthy manner, motivation and goals can lead to great accomplishments and pride in one's work. However, unhealthy perfectionistic behaviors can lead to tears, frustration, anxiety, distress, underachievement, and even depression. The joy of learning and trying new things is nonexistent for those experiencing unhealthy perfectionism. Again, if your child or a student in your class seems to be experiencing extreme unhealthy perfectionism—or if their perfectionism is affecting their eating and sleeping habits, causing them to be withdrawn or resulting in other signs of depression—we encourage you to seek the advice of a professional, such as a counselor or psychologist.

Figure 9 provides some signs of unhealthy perfectionism that indicate that you may wish to begin conversations with the child and utilize some of the other strategies suggested in this book (see Chapters 9 and 10 in particular), as the child might need to redirect their perfectionism and use it in a healthier manner.

Characteristics of Healthy Motivation and Goals

Although families and educators often do not think about children's motivation unless it is being manifested in unhealthy ways, such as stress, unhappiness, tears, procrastination, isolation, or fear, it also is important to recognize that motivation and goals can be used in healthy ways, leading to high achievement, personal satisfaction, improvement, and productivity. Children who exhibit perfectionistic behaviors need to have their standards and goals validated by their educators and family members rather than being chastised for having standards that are "too high." Having high goals and standards is healthy for children if they recognize that it takes time, effort, and revision and practice to reach their goals and that they will make mistakes along the way. By setting short-term and **intermediate goals**, children are able to maintain their high standards but work toward them at a reasonable pace. Although children should work to improve by revising their work and practicing their skills, they also should maintain balance by not sacrificing sleep or other healthy habits, including making

FIGURE 9
Signs of Unhealthy Perfectionism

1. The child takes no joy in the process (is only focused on outcomes).
2. The child avoids challenges and risks (only engages in activities in which they are confident they will succeed).
3. The child is fixated on redoing work because it never meets their own standards.
4. The child makes elaborate plans for an end product but has difficulty starting the product or project.
5. The child hides their mistakes.
6. The child cheats in order to win (in academics, sports, or games).
7. The child cries or becomes otherwise upset when confronted with an error.
8. The child makes excuses rather than admitting a fault or mistake.
9. The child views even small mistakes as catastrophic (e.g., a potential A- is described as "failing a test").
10. The child is overly focused on precision.
11. The child constantly evaluates themselves.
12. The child becomes frustrated when something does not come easily.
13. Life is unbalanced because the child is overly focused on perfection in one area.
14. The child has strained relationships with their peers due to high expectations.
15. The child struggles in competitive situations, creating excuses or quitting if a win is not inevitable.

time for themselves and for activity and socialization. To use their motivation in a healthy way, children need to recognize opportunities to learn from their mistakes and must move their focus from reaching perfection to improving and reaching specific goals through effort and revision.

Learning how to transform unhealthy perfectionism into healthy motivation and goals takes time and dedication. Figure 10 provides a list of skills that can help develop healthy motivation and goals in children.

> *High standards are not necessarily unhealthy. People need to have high standards that they work to achieve through practice and revision.*

Tools to Identify Perfectionism

As described in Chapter 2, there are several formal instruments that are used in research and clinical settings to identify perfectionism in children and adults. School counselors, gifted education professionals, and trained therapists and psychologists often have access to these instruments. Also, they often are available by contacting the researchers who developed the instrument. In addition to instruments that are developed specifically to identify perfectionism, many assessments of psychological distress contain measures of unhealthy perfectionism. These instruments may be used to diagnose perfectionistic tendencies that may be hindering your child's emotional well-being.

Informal assessments, as opposed to more **formal assessments**, made through anecdotal records kept by family members and educators may be just as useful in identifying areas, situations, and ways in which a child exhibits perfectionistic tendencies. Many families and educators find it helpful to keep a journal to record incidents in which a child may be exhibiting unhealthy perfectionistic behaviors. This type of information can help to detect patterns of behavior and may aid adults in identifying helpful strategies for changing behavior.

Final Thoughts

Although most people tend to view perfectionism as a primarily negative trait, having high standards and motivation can be healthy and productive. Educators and families can help children change unhealthy behaviors into more positive traits. Perfectionism can be identified through

FIGURE 10
Skills for Building Healthy Motivation and Goals

1. The child sets realistic short-term, intermediate, and long-term goals.
2. The child has high standards for performance.
3. The child focuses on improvement rather than on being flawless on the first attempt.
4. The child is driven by intrinsic motivation.
5. The child focuses on effort.
6. The child celebrates personal successes.
7. The child revises and redoes work without obsessing about minor flaws.
8. The child learns from their mistakes.
9. The child takes risks.
10. The child enjoys trying new challenges.

various formal instruments or through informal records kept by educators and families. These records can be used to identify patterns of behavior and possible strategies to help young perfectionists use their perfectionism in healthy ways.

CHAPTER 9

Strategies for the Classroom

Educators play many roles and face many challenges in their classroom. Although not all of their students exhibit perfectionistic behaviors, all educators can share stories about students they have taught who struggle with unhealthy perfectionism. Moreover, if they were to observe their students carefully throughout the day and in multiple scenarios, such as during class, at recess, and in music or art, educators might see more examples of unhealthy perfectionism than they even realized. For instance, the five types of perfectionism we have defined are based on observing just one fourth-grade class. In this chapter, we present an overview of the strategies we presented for each type of perfectionist (see Table 6 for more detail). Then, we share general strategies to use motivation and goals in a healthy way rather than the perfectionistic tendencies and behaviors that are unhealthy, followed by activities to use in the classroom. Although some strategies require more one-on-one or small-group work with students, perhaps during quarterly one-on-one conferences, others can be done with the entire class and would benefit all students.

TABLE 6
Strategies to Promote Healthy Perfectionism in the Classroom

Type of Perfectionist	Strategies to Use
Academic Achievers	• Praise efforts and products rather than focusing on high grades; focus on efforts and strategies rather than on "being smart" and earning good grades • Guide students in taking pride in the process and how to use mistakes as learning experiences • Use diagnostic testing and discuss its purposes with students • Use formative assessments as an opportunity to learn from mistakes and recognize strengths (mastery) and weaknesses
Aggravated Accuracy Assessors	• Recognize students' standards as acceptable and valuable as long-term goals and have faith in their vision and ability to meet expectations through revision and effort • Help students reframe unrealistic immediate or short-term goals as medium- or long-term goals • Facilitate a discussion on balance with parents and students • Read and discuss successful people whose success depended on revisions • Focus on process and improvement rather than the end product • Use constructive criticism and critique as a classroom tool, including setting goals for improvement • Provide opportunities for rough drafts and for polished work

TABLE 6, continued

Type of Perfectionist	Strategies to Use
Risk Evaders	• Develop a safe classroom environment that encourages risk-taking • Encourage students to try new challenges within this safe environment • Provide opportunities for smaller risks that do not guarantee success • Applaud students for effort and trying new challenges, redefining "success" • Help students focus on process and revisions rather than final product or outcome • Have students set future goals after a risk-taking event or task
Controlling Image Managers	• Use small-group role-playing to address social issues that arise in competitive situations at school • Read and discuss losses of role models in competitive situations • Invite guest speakers to share their personal defeats and their focus on improvement • Help students set personal goals based on their performance rather than on comparisons with peers • Encourage students and applaud them for trying challenging, competitive situations and taking risks • Applaud students for effort and risk-taking
Procrastinating Perfectionists	• Help students break down projects into smaller tasks and develop a schedule with "buffers" • Work with students to prioritize • Address fear of failure • Focus on process and effort rather than outcomes and products • Focus on success along the way, rather than just at the final deadline or event

General Strategies to Promote Healthy Motivation and Goals in the Classroom and to Create a Supportive Environment

Throughout the five chapters focusing on the different types of perfectionistic behaviors and tendencies, several recommendations held true for many of the types. The most important recommendation we can make for educators is to create a safe environment for risk-taking and for learning from mistakes. Students should feel supported in the challenges they attempt and should not face ridicule from their classmates or others for trying something new. Just as you model **metacognition** and help students think about their learning, you should model risk-taking and learning from mistakes. For instance, you might share during a **morning meeting** that you are taking a photography class and the challenges you are facing. (For a book on morning meetings, see Chapter 12.) You might choose to participate in a P.E., art, or music lesson, letting the students know that you are going outside your comfort zone and trying something new along with the students. When you make a mistake on the board, do not just erase it and move on. Instead, make students aware that you, and they, cannot be perfect and that mistakes do happen.

> *Creating an environment that is safe for risk-taking and that encourages learning from mistakes is essential for students to use their motivation in a healthy way.*

Setting this necessary culture and climate of acceptance and safe risk-taking should begin with the first day of school. It is never too late to work with students to create this climate, but the earlier in the year it is established, the easier it is for students to accept it and for it to be natural. A book that we have used with children is *Be a Perfect Person in Just Three Days!* by Stephen Manes. This is a great read-aloud during the first week or so of school. In the story, the main character, Milo, reads a book and follows steps to become perfect in just 3 days, including wearing a stalk of broccoli around his neck for a full day. In the end, he learns that being perfect is just not fun. This book can lead to immediate discussions about perfectionism and also gives a reference point for the future. For example, when you make a mistake, you can jokingly suggest a student get a stalk of broccoli for you to wear. Similar references with students might help defuse a situation in which they are emotionally overwhelmed by a mistake they have made or a challenge they are struggling with.

To help your class create an environment safe for risk-taking that creates a community that works together, we recommend you spend the first couple days of school with some planned risk-taking activities and other noncompetitive or cooperative activities. Some examples are included in the following sections.

Games and Cooperative Activities

Jill took some time each day to play a class game of kickball, with the goal of students supporting each other and learning the sport. She discussed the purpose and explained that some students had never played baseball or kickball before. Those who were already on baseball or softball teams naturally took on a mentoring role and would cheer for and explain the rules to their peers trying the game for the first time. The score was not the issue—learning to play as a class was the goal. (Jill purposefully chose teams so that they each would have a mix of novices and advanced players.)

Another cooperative activity that gets students to interact together is the human knot. To do this, have about eight students gather in a tight circle (you will need to use multiple groups for this so that the groups are not too large). Then, have them put their right hand into the middle of the circle and hold someone else's hand (not someone immediately next to them). Next, they put in their left hand and hold another person's hand (again, not someone next to them, or the person they held hands with before). The students then have to untangle their knot without letting go.

Relay races and field day-type activities provide another fun opportunity for risk, especially if you do silly events that challenge the athletic students and give nonathletic students a chance. This provides risk for everyone and allows students to focus on having fun and working together. For instance, you could do the following activities with your class:

- **"Pass the roll" game:** Have the students stand in a line all facing the same direction. Give the first person a ball, a roll of toilet paper, or similar object. They have to pass the object under their legs to the person behind them, who then passes the object over their head to the person behind them, who then passes it under their legs, and so on until it reaches the end. With toilet paper, you can have the students actually unroll it and try not to break the chain. You can do this competitively (2–3 lines of students trying to do this task as quickly as possible), or you can time your class and challenge them to talk together about how to improve their time before they repeat the activity.

- **Egg and spoon relay:** Divide the class into several teams. Have them run a relay race with an egg on a spoon.
- **Five-legged race:** Have the students run a five-legged race (teams of four instead of partners). Then combine two groups continuously until the whole class is walking together.
- **Hula-hoop race:** Have the class stand in a circle holding hands. Separate two students' hands, place a hula-hoop there, and have them hold hands again. Now have the class get the hula-hoop all of the way around the circle. Once they get going, add another hula-hoop and then a third. Once students have those going really well, add a hula-hoop of another color and have it go in the opposite direction.

Art Activities

Take some time to do creative art activities and then have students practice critiquing their work, pointing out what they really like about the work and what they think would make the work more interesting. This section includes some projects that are fun and relax students' standards (because art can bring out many perfectionistic tendencies).

Have students look at some Sumi-e Japanese ink paintings. On the Japan Objects website (https://japanobjects.com/features/sumie), Sato (2020) does a nice job describing the painting of nature not as copying reality but as recreating it in your own conception. This idea gives students freedom not to try to capture every detail precisely as seen. Other aspects of the aesthetics of Japanese painting that should be discussed include simplicity of line and color and elegance of technique.

To create their own paintings, first have students create a tissue paper collage background. To do this, give each student a piece of heavy white paper that is approximately 4 inches by 4 inches. Have them tear pieces of tissue paper into strips that are 1/2 inch to 1 inch high and 4 inches long. Mix a proportion of 3 parts water to 1 part white glue into cups. Then, have the students paint the white paper with the glue mixture and place the tissue paper strips on top. Warm colors (red, yellow, and orange) can go on the top of the paper to represent a sunset or sunrise. Cool colors (blue, violet, and green) can go on the bottom to represent the ground. It is best if the warm and cool colors do not mix. As the students lay each piece of tissue paper on the white paper, they should paint over the tissue paper with the glue mixture to secure it. The tissue paper should overlap slightly. Once the strips of tissue paper have dried, they can begin to add the Sumi-e painting on top. One nonthreatening way to do this is to use straws and India ink to create a tree-like shape. India ink is inexpensive and can be found at most art supplies stores; however, black tempera paint mixed with water also will work for this project. Have the students lay their tissue paper paintings on the table on top of a larger piece of newspaper. They should move so that their face is level with the top of the table. Place a few drops of India ink on their paper and have the students blow the ink on their paper using a straw. They may want to practice this technique on some scrap paper before trying it out on their project. Let their trees dry overnight. (See Figure 11 for examples.)

Once students have created their Sumi-e paintings and allowed them to dry, create a gallery, and then have students critique the paintings. First, have them describe what is similar in all of the paintings. Then have them share what stands out in certain paintings that draw viewers to those particular ones. Finally, have them talk with a partner and share one thing they would do differently in their own work next time they do it. Because this is their first time critiquing, sharing with only a partner and sharing what they would change rather than what someone else would change allows students to become comfortable with this side of critiquing before having others give suggestions for improvement. As students get more involved in critiquing, suggestions from the Kennedy Center are a good place to start (see https://www.kennedy-center.org/education/resources-for-educators/ classroom-resources/articles-and-how-tos/articles/educators/teaching-students-to-critique). To read about integrating this activity and other activities in language arts, see the article "Art Across the Curriculum: Language Arts" (Wilson & Adelson, 2008).

Risk-taking in school often begins with putting pencil on paper. For another fun art activity, distribute a sheet of paper with squiggles drawn on it (like the ones in Figure 12). Give students a set amount of time (2–3 minutes usually is good) to transform the squiggles into something. Have them share. Discuss which drawing is the most original and which is the most elaborate.

FIGURE 11
Sumi-E Painting Examples Created by Lily, Age 7

Challenge Activities

Give students opportunities to take academic risks as well. Provide an extension activity in mathematics, science, language arts, and social studies that will challenge them. Have each student choose one challenge to do that week. Be sure it is something that is not routine and that will challenge them. At the end of the week, have students share whether they were able to solve or complete the challenge, what they found challenging about it, and how they persisted. Be sure to define success as having tried the challenge and focus on applauding effort rather than completing or solving the challenge.

Give students a colored index card. Have them write down something they have never tried before (academic, athletic, or artistic) but would like to and have the means to try in a week (cannot take months to prepare for, be too costly, involve unattainable or unavailable equipment, be out of season, etc.). Some examples might be to try inline skating for the first time (borrowing a pair of skates from a friend), to try playing a sister's guitar, to try scrapbooking, to learn multiplication with decimals, to jump rope 200 times without missing a jump, to write a children's picture book, to learn the capitals of all of the states, to draw a self-portrait, or to conduct a particular science experiment. Post the challenges on a bulletin board and have students attempt a challenge as a homework assignment due the next week. Again, emphasize that the goal is to try it. Have students report back

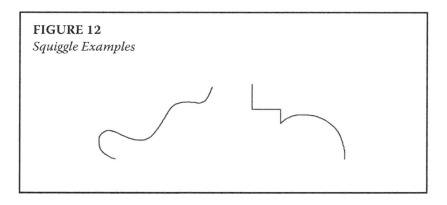

FIGURE 12
Squiggle Examples

or write a journal entry about what they tried, their emotions when trying something new, and what challenge they would like to try next.

Creating a Safe Environment

You also might consider having a morning meeting each day. This can be just a 10–15-minute period in which you and the students greet one another and do an activity or discuss an issue together. Although we understand that time in school is stretched with many demands, this is time well-spent in the classroom because it helps establish a community and helps both the educator and students address issues in a safe place rather than having these issues impact the entire day. If you want more information about morning meetings, we recommend *The Morning Meeting Book* by Roxann Kriete. (See Chapter 12 for more information on this book.)

One key to supporting perfectionists and creating a safe environment for them to take risks and learn from mistakes is to address issues as they arrive rather than letting them build, and morning meetings gives an opportunity for this to happen. After students greet one another (perhaps by tossing a foam ball to a person while greeting them in a different language or by practicing "professional" handshakes to greet neighbors), you might consider allowing two or three students to share an accomplishment, helping them focus on improvement and effort or a challenge that they faced and what happened. This would be a good time for role-playing activities as well, especially as you notice issues arising at recess, in the lunchroom, or during group work. This also might be an ideal time to have students set goals for the day, week, or marking period. At the beginning of each marking period, you might give students a colored index card and have them write three **concrete goals** focused on their own performance (not comparisons) and three steps they will take to meet those goals. These can be taped to the corner of their desk to remind them of their goals.

In general, you will want to be very aware of the language you use and the message you send to your students. Encourage students to try and to take risks, and let them know that they are not always expected to succeed on their first try. Ease students' fears before an assessment, and debrief with them after the assessment, letting them know the next steps for the class based on the results.

> *Your words are powerful—be supportive of children and focus on their efforts, improvement, and the learning process, rather than just on outcomes and final products.*

Most importantly, shift your focus to your students' efforts and improvements rather than just their mastery of curriculum. As educators, we want students to master particular skills and content to be successful in life and to meet state and national standards. However, to help students reach mastery, we must focus on their efforts and improvements. This will help all students. For instance, our gifted and talented students often are short-changed in the current focus on standards, mastery, and meeting a level of proficiency. By focusing more on improvement, these students will continue to be challenged and learn more, even if they enter our classrooms already proficient at grade-level objectives. Moreover, as you focus on students' efforts and improvements, recognizing students for these rather than primarily for outcomes like grades, your students will take pride in their efforts and will shift their own focus to evaluating themselves on whether they have improved or not. With a focus on improvement, mastery will come! For instance, when testing students on multiplication facts, provide students with a score indicating improvement rather than number right or wrong. So, if Joey correctly answered three more problems this time than the last time, you would write "+3" on his paper. This gives students a much more tangible, realistic short-term goal—to improve steadily—rather than an overwhelming picture of needing to master all of the facts. This also can lend itself to graphing, so that students see the upward trend as they learn more and more.

A strategy particularly useful for Procrastinating Perfectionists but one that all students would benefit from is time management and breaking larger tasks into smaller subtasks. These study skills will become increasingly important as students get older and have more responsibilities. Having your students use an agenda/planner is a great method to help them take ownership for their learning, to help them make a plan for what they need to accomplish at home each evening and throughout the week, and to communicate with families. We have seen students as young as kindergarten and first grade benefit from writing their homework in an agenda each day. If the school adopts a policy for all students to use agendas or planners (with different formats for primary and intermediate students), students begin at an early age to develop these skills and can refine them as they get older and have more long-term projects and assignments. Be sure that students write in time to study for tests and work on projects prior to the night before the test. Personal and extracurricular goals also should be included in this process. Set goals for spending a set amount of time or studying a particular topic each night leading up to the test so that students feel prepared and do not procrastinate, staying up late the night before. In some cases, writing in free time or planned activities, such as soccer practice or piano lessons, can be helpful to students to see how they can manage their school tasks and still enjoy their other commitments or hobbies. In your morning meeting, you should address the importance of sleep and why preparing for a test or working on a project prior to the night before (or starting homework 20 minutes before bedtime) is harmful to students' future performance and learning.

Activities to Use in the Classroom

Children spend many hours in school and are being formally and informally evaluated by educators, themselves, and their peers on an ongoing basis. Many types of perfectionistic behaviors are exhibited within the classroom, and classroom practices can lead to students exhibiting both healthy motivation and goals and unhealthy perfectionistic tendencies. This is particularly true for children who are "schoolhouse" gifted (Renzulli, 1986) and who build their personal identity on their school accomplishments and interactions.

> *Children constantly are evaluated in schools—use this as a time to help students use their motivation in a healthy way rather than persisting in unhealthy perfectionistic tendencies.*

Within Existing Activities

One way that educators can encourage healthy motivation and goal setting in the classroom is through an approach that emphasizes learning from mistakes and allows for revisions. Most educators naturally focus on the revision process when it comes to writing, but children, particularly those in upper elementary school and middle school who receive grades on their report card, need to know that there is more to learning than getting a certain grade or percent correct. Formal assessments, including both diagnostic tests (or pretests) and summative tests (or posttests), provide an opportunity to teach children about the purposes of school and learning and to remove the focus from the final grade and perfection. This is a chance to teach children that learning is an ongoing process and that assessment is meant to help educators and students determine what the students have learned and what areas they need to improve.

Diagnostic Testing (Pretesting)

Diagnostic testing is an important tool for educators interested in differentiation, **curriculum compacting**, and measuring student growth. It allows the educator and students to determine which areas of a topic each student already has mastered and where the child is developmentally or conceptually so that the educator can plan learning activities accordingly. However, diagnostic tests can be a daunting task for perfectionists, particularly the Academic Achievers. Educators need to talk explicitly with students about the diagnostic nature of pretests, explaining what they are used for and communicating that students should not know everything on these tests. Encouraging students to write a question mark or IDK (which stands for, "I don't know") rather than leave a question blank eases some of the pressure off them as they have *something* to write on the paper and they know that this is acceptable.

Another useful activity with students is to give them the opportunity to compare their posttest (**summative assessment**) results with their pretest results, particularly focusing on concepts that students mastered during the unit. This reframes the goal of learning from the end grade to growth and improvement, removing the pressure to achieve 100% and focusing more on progress. Educators and families can help students make this transition by having them reflect on what they learned during the unit and helping them set goals based on the posttest. Having children reflect on what they think they should learn or what they want to learn next, using the posttest to support their reflections, gives them the opportunity to see that continued growth, to understand the goals of continued learning and that the test is not the ultimate goal, and to identify their own strengths and weaknesses.

Summative Assessments (Posttests)

Another way of helping children see the usefulness of assessment beyond just a final grade is to use the posttest as a learning tool. For instance, in math, after the teacher has graded students' posttests, the teacher should spend a class period having students correct any problems they missed. However, educators must keep in mind that this activity still has the potential to have students focus on right and wrong. One way to help them focus more on learning from their mistakes is to have them fold their paper in half vertically ("hot dog style"). The left column is labeled "Correct Answer." In this space, students show their work and find the correct answer. The right column is labeled **"WIMI,"** which stands for **"Why I Missed It."** Students then explain what mistake they made. This helps students focus on concepts and process—for example, noting whether they did not understand a particular concept or whether they made a careless error in their arithmetic. The entire class works on helping all students master any problems that they did not answer correctly on the posttest. Students work together to teach each other missed concepts and help each other find their mistakes. When a student has corrected all of their missed problems and explained why they missed those problems, that student becomes an "expert" on the topic and is available for other students to consult. The WIMI method works very well with mathematics because it involves concepts, process, content, and skills. Students can really analyze their work and learn from the answer they originally indicated and the correct answer. This approach could be modified in other subject areas, depending on the type of assessment and the material assessed. Figure 13 provides an example of WIMI used with a mathematics assessment.

FIGURE 13

WIMI Example

The take-home message for educators is to have students immediately address mistakes, misconceptions, and unlearned concepts and to learn from the posttest itself. Depending on the topic as well as on the results, the educator might consider creating small groups to address particular concepts or skills together, explaining how students were chosen for the group (using the data from the posttest), and then providing an opportunity for students to demonstrate their growth since the posttest through either a formal or informal assessment. Again, the educator must explicitly have students examine their growth from the posttest to this new assessment. Otherwise, students may not realize the growth they have made and may continue to focus on the end product (the test) and their lack of perfection on the product.

Sometimes students are so focused on the final grade for a test that they lose sight of what they have learned during a particular unit of study or marking period. As mentioned before, comparing results and responses from a pretest and posttest is one strategy to help students better see what they have learned. Another strategy involves students directly reflecting on what they have learned. Before a unit, have students write in their journals, create a **mind map**, or record in another way what they already know about the topic, and collect these responses. At the end of the unit, have them repeat the exercise, and then return their original recording so that they can compare and see the growth they have made. Even just having students take a moment at the end of the test to respond to a question such as, "What are three things you learned during this unit that you did not know before?" or "What do you think you have improved on most during this unit?" (for a more skills-based unit) allows them the opportunity to reflect on their improvement and learning rather than just judge themselves by a grade. Some educators prefer to use K-W-L (What I Know, What I Want to Know, What I Have Learned) charts in their classrooms. These charts also can be used to measure what students know and learn about a topic, and they are easy ways for students to see how their knowledge has progressed from the beginning of the unit.

Constructive Criticism and Feedback

Students need opportunities to reflect on their strengths and areas to improve (a more positive term than *weaknesses*) and to become comfortable with the fact that others will see high-quality aspects as well as flaws in all products that they produce. The earlier educators engage students in critiquing their own work as well as the work of their peers, the more comfortable they can become with this fact and with the process of improvement. At the end of a major project or performance, have students use a rubric to reflect on how they did. This rubric could be created by the educator, by individual students, or as a whole-class activity. For primary students, rubrics can rely on visual images (e.g., smiley faces) rather than words. The resources section of this book (Chapter 12) provides several resources for educators on the development of rubrics and websites with sample rubrics. On each rubric, be sure to include an open-response section in which students have to identify at least two or three strengths that they are proud of in their work as well as two or three areas that they would like to improve the next time they do a similar project (see the rubric in Figure 14). This can be related to details in the project itself, such as their attention to detail, the content knowledge that was acquired and represented, or their improvement in a particular skill, or it can be related to the process, such as their time management, their collaborative skills, or their use of the library and other resources. If you do not have time to conference with each of your students, having them do peer critiques is an alternative

FIGURE 14
Sample Rubric

Social Studies Review Game Rubric

Category	Excellent	Good	Needs Improvement	Below Expectations	Student Score	Teacher Score
Accuracy of Content	All questions and answers made for the game are correct. (Up to 32 points)	All but one of the questions and answers for the game are correct. (Up to 24 points)	All but two of the questions and answers for the game are correct. (Up to 16 points)	Several questions and answers for the game are not accurate. (Up to 8 points)		
Met Question Guidelines	Included the minimum number of questions for each category. (Up to 28 points)	Included the minimum number of questions for all but one category. (Up to 21 points)	Included the minimum number of questions for all but two categories. (Up to 14 points)	Did not include the minimum number of questions for more than two categories. (Up to 7 points)		
Rules	Rules were written clearly enough that all could easily participate. (Up to 12 points)	Rules were written, but one part of the game needed slightly more explanation. (Up to 9 points)	Rules were written, but people had some difficulty figuring out the game. (Up to 6 points)	The rules were not written. (Up to 3 points)		

FIGURE 14, continued

Category	Excellent	Good	Needs Improvement	Below Expectations	Student Score	Teacher Score
Timeliness	All components were submitted on time (work plan with dates, draft questions and answers, game). (Up to 16 points)	One component was submitted no more than 2 days late. All other components submitted on time. (Up to 12 points)	Two components were submitted no more than 2 days late, and a third component was submitted on time. (Up to 9 points)	A component was submitted more than 2 days late, or all components were late. (Up to 6 points)		
Final Product	The board is colorful, attractive, and not messy. The questions and answers are legible. The rules are typed or written very neatly. The materials are present and stored in a convenient way. (Up to 8 points)	One of the major components (board, questions and answers, rules, materials) does not meet the standards and distracts from game play. (Up to 6 points)	Two of the major components (board, questions and answers, rules, materials) do not meet the standards and distract from game play. (Up to 4 points)	Three of the major components (board, questions and answers, rules, materials) do not meet the standards and distract from game play. -OR- A major component interferes with the game being able to be played. (Up to 2 points)		

FIGURE 14, continued

Category	Excellent	Good	Needs Improvement	Below Expectations	Student Score	Teacher Score
Creativity	A lot of thought went into making the game interesting and fun to play, as shown by creative questions, game pieces, and/or game board. (Up to 4 points)	Some thought went into making the game interesting and fun to play, as shown by using textures, fancy writing, and/or interesting characters. (Up to 3 points)	The student tried to make the game interesting and fun, but some of the elements made it harder to understand/enjoy the game. (Up to 2 points)	Little thought was put into making the game interesting or fun. (Up to 1 point)		

Student reflection: Reflect on your project and the process of making it. On the back, write 2–3 things you did well. Then, write two things you could improve. These can be about a component of the game itself, your planning, or your time management.

way for them to discuss with someone else their strengths and the areas in which they need to improve. The "Mathematician to Mathematician" worksheet in Figure 15 is an example of how students might be guided to identify strengths and areas for improvement in their classmates' work.

Estimating, Hypothesizing, and Predicting

As an educator, you know these are important skills for students in many content areas, including mathematics, science, and the arts. However, these also are great opportunities to address perfectionistic tendencies with students. When students estimate, hypothesize, or predict, have them write in pen or marker so that they cannot erase what they wrote when they find out the "right answer." Talk with students about why we do these processes and about learning from them. For instance, when we "guess and test" in mathematics, our goal is to refine our "guess" each time, based on the results from when we tested the previous guess—we learn from what we did and continue. Students need to know that they are not expected to know the answer before a science experiment, before solving a mathematics problem, or before mixing colors or trying a new technique in art. We have experiences so that we can learn—if students already knew all of the answers, what fun would life be? There would be no joy in learning, and we want our students to experience that joy of discovery.

Specific Activities Addressing Perfectionistic Behaviors

Not only does writing naturally lend itself to opportunities to address revision and process, but it also allows an outlet for students to reflect on perfectionism and for educators to encourage healthy expressions of motivation and high goals and standards for oneself. One common pitfall for unhealthy perfectionists is that they focus on their mistakes and equate mistakes to failure. Although discussions about learning from mistakes and reading about those who have made mistakes and learned from them throughout history (such as Thomas Edison and Leonardo da Vinci) provide an intellectual understanding for perfectionists, students need to integrate this perspective of mistakes as learning experiences. One easy way to have students reflect on a healthy view of mistakes is to have them create an acrostic poem. On the left side of the paper, the student writes

FIGURE 15
Mathematician to Mathematician Worksheet

Mathematician to Mathematician

Please complete the following to provide feedback to your partner about her or his writing. Remember that good mathematical writing includes:

- The answers to all questions;
- Mathematical vocabulary;
- Reasons that back up the parts of your solution;
- And maybe representations (like tables, graphs, pictures, numbers, and equations).

This Stands Out!
Describe the one positive characteristic that really stood out in your partner's writing.
Words That Describe
List any vocabulary words your partner can use to make his or her thinking more clear.
Clearing Up the Mathematical Thinking
Write any questions that may help your partner make her or his response more clear. Consider starting your questions with phrases like: "Tell me more about . . .", "What do you mean when you say . . .?", "What else did you think about after you . . . and before you . . .?", and "Think about using a [representation] to show . . ."
Continue Doing This!
Describe any other features from your partner's writing that he or she did well.

Note. Developed by Dr. Tutita M. Casa, Project M³: Mentoring Mathematical Minds, University of Connecticut. Reprinted with permission.

the letters M-I-S-T-A-K-E-S. Then, they write a word or sentence (depending on what the teacher or student chooses as the format) starting with each of those letters, focusing on how mistakes are learning opportunities. Several examples are included in Figures 16, 17, and 18.

> *Teaching process skills is an excellent opportunity to emphasize that there are moments when perfection is not expected!*

Not only can this activity be used as a reflection piece that solidifies what children are learning, but it also serves as a reminder to students when they do get upset about mistakes. Moreover, educators can use this activity as a diagnostic tool, finding out how students view mistakes prior to addressing unhealthy fixation on mistakes and imperfections.

Journal writing can be cathartic for students, and it can help you identify issues that need to be addressed. You can have students write as a morning activity, a quiet time after lunch before moving into the afternoon lessons, or as a means to practice their grammar and spelling. Some possible journal topics include the following: responding to scenarios, setting goals and plans to reach those goals, and reflecting on how they felt before, during, and after a particular risk-taking or challenging experience. Additionally, providing quotes for students to respond to can help them think about some important issues related to perfectionism. Some quotes you might consider using include the following:

- "Forget mistakes. Forget failure. Forget everything except what you're going to do now and do it. Today is your lucky day."—Will Durant
- "If you're trying to achieve, there will be roadblocks. I've had them; everybody has had them. But obstacles don't have to stop you. If you run into a wall, don't turn around and give up. Figure out how to climb it, go through it, or work around it."—Michael Jordan
- "Fear is a part of everything you do . . . You have to take great risks to get big rewards."—Greg Louganis
- "Do one thing every day that scares you."—Eleanor Roosevelt
- "Striving for excellence motivates you; striving for perfection is demoralizing."—Harriet Braiker
- "Certain flaws are necessary for the whole. It would seem strange if old friends lacked certain quirks."—Goethe

FIGURE 16
MISTAKE Acrostic Poem by Hayley of Newport News, VA

Making a mistake isn't a catastrophical thing.

If you don't believe me, you should see the pile of crumpled papers next to me.

So if you make a mistake, correct it and move on.

There is no such thing as perfection.

Although we strive for perfection, we can only try our best.

Kryptonite is Superman's weakness, and we all have our own

Embrace your mistakes and learn from your experiences.

So quit trying to be perfect because mistakes add character.

- "No one is perfect; that is why pencils have erasers."—Unknown
- "A man would do nothing if he waited until he could do it so well that no one could find fault."—John Henry Newman

Especially as students enter the upper elementary grades, they are able to articulate their feelings. As you model learning from mistakes, taking risks, setting goals, and focusing on effort and improvement, students also take on these behaviors and develop their own strategies for using perfectionism in a healthy way. Many students are eager to share what they have learned and to help other students. Consider giving students an outlet to do this. Suggest to the art teacher that when students are learn-

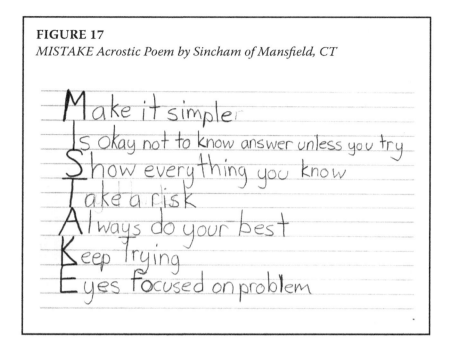

FIGURE 17
MISTAKE Acrostic Poem by Sincham of Mansfield, CT

Make it simpler
Is okay not to know answer unless you try
Show everything you know
Take a risk
Always do your best
Keep Trying
Eyes focused on problem

ing a new technique they be encouraged to create some art expressing a strategy they find useful when they are worried about a big project, test, or performance. Give students an opportunity to write a play or a puppet show for younger students about some of the issues you have discussed in morning meetings, such as trying a new challenge, playing fairly in games, or goal setting. Students also might enjoy writing and/or illustrating children's stories about some of these issues. You could use *Nobody's Perfect: A Story for Children About Perfectionism* by Ellen Flanagan Burns as an example. You also can have students rewrite the endings to books, stories, or biographical accounts you read, perhaps noting how the endings might have changed had everything not worked out in the protagonist's favor.

Bibliotherapy and **videotherapy** are other tools that you can use in your classroom to address perfectionism. They introduce children to characters with similar problems (Adderholdt-Elliott & Eller, 1989; Wimberley et al., 2016). According to Hébert (1991, 2009), the world of fiction, whether it be through books or movies, offers safe places for exploration, discussion, and evaluation of the behaviors of protagonists and other characters who may reflect a child's own interests, problems, and concerns. By

---

FIGURE 18
MISTAKE Acrostic Poem Compiled From Poems
by Students in Mrs. Nancy Titchen's Class

M aking mistakes is a great way to learn.

I f you don't make mistakes, you won't learn a lot.

S tay positive and tell yourself you can do it.

T ry to fix your mistake and learn from it.

m **A** kes you feel more relaxed and willing to try it again.

be **K** ind to yourself; everyone makes mistakes.

E ven Albert Einstein made mistakes.

Note. This compilation is composed from poems by Joseph, Melania, Michael, and Tim of Mansfield, CT.

---

selecting particular books and movies that feature children who exhibit perfectionistic behaviors (see Chapter 11 for some suggestions), you provide a common situation to open a dialogue with students to address perfectionism in the classroom. By using bibliotherapy or videotherapy, you can help students identify and address issues before they become problems (Wimberley et al., 2016). In addition to stimulating discussions about issues related to perfectionism, the use of bibliotherapy and videotherapy might make your students aware that other children have similar issues and help them identify realistic situations and articulate their own feelings. Frasier and McCannon (1981) indicated that bibliotherapy can be used in four ways in the classroom: to address an entire class problem (such as preparing for the state assessment), to address an individual problem that affects the entire class (such as Controlling Image Managers quitting during competitive situations), to address small-group problems (such as working with just Academic Achievers), and to address personal problems (such as "the development of a positive view of oneself;" p. 82). Once students have read the book or watched the video, there are many options for follow-up activities, including the following:

- in-depth discussions that focus on a particular character and their perfectionistic behaviors;
- an art activity, such as a collage illustrating the character's perfectionistic behaviors or a comic strip of how the character would react in a situation because they have a perfectionistic tendencies;
- creative writing, such as writing a different resolution to a situation in which the character exhibited perfectionist tendencies or writing an internal dialogue of a character's perfectionistic thoughts;
- drama, such as role-playing, reconstructing perfectionistic behaviors with puppets, or creating and enacting a new scene with the same characters in other situations;
- creative problem solving, graphic organizers, and other tools (be creative and let your students be creative); and
- mindfulness activities.

> *We know time in school is precious— integrate activities addressing perfectionism into your regular curriculum.*

Take opportunities to integrate activities specifically addressing perfectionism into your regular curriculum. Just as it is good practice to integrate different content areas, students benefit greatly when you integrate aspects of social-emotional health with academic activities. For instance, when studying famous people, such as historical figures or particular scientists, do not have students only research their contribution to history or science. Instead, also have students learn about them as people—have them research what mistakes they made, how they dealt with them, and what risks they took. Not only will students be learning social-emotional skills, but this also will humanize these figures from the past, which will help students become more interested in them and retain more information about their contributions.

Final Thoughts

When addressing unhealthy perfectionistic behaviors and tendencies in the classroom, setting up a safe classroom environment is vital.

Additionally, specific classroom activities, such as journal writing and morning meeting sessions, may help move children from unhealthy perfectionistic behaviors to healthy motivation. Educators also have found that having students reflect on the process of creating their final products, especially through the use of rubrics, can help reduce unhealthy perfectionistic tendencies in their students.

CHAPTER 10

Strategies for the Home

Families often are perplexed by the behaviors of their children who are demonstrating perfectionistic tendencies. There are few things more frustrating to the caregiver of a child than the meltdowns, arguments, and anguish that can accompany perfectionism. However, there are some strategies available for families to help their children cope and use their motivation and high standards in a healthy way. In this chapter, we offer both advice for the "crisis moment" in which unhealthy perfectionistic behaviors and tendencies are rearing their ugly heads, as well as strategies to use in general to help children change unhealthy perfectionism into healthy motivation and goals. Table 7 summarizes the strategies discussed in the previous chapters to offer help in the home for each type of perfectionistic tendencies.

Throughout the previous sections, we have suggested strategies specific to each type of perfectionistic tendency. The guiding principles behind these strategies, such as discussion with children, encouraging healthy habits, and increased family activities underlie many of the examples and activities here as well. However, be sure that if you feel that your

TABLE 7
Strategies to Promote Healthy Perfectionism in the Home

Type of Perfectionist	Strategies to Use
Academic Achievers	• Deemphasize grades • Celebrate learning and growth • Be an example in your mistakes • Choose books and movies to illustrate "flawed protagonists" • Find off-peak times to talk to your children
Aggravated Accuracy Assessors	• Help children set goals in multiple areas of life • Distinguish between realistic and unrealistic goals • Distinguish between short-, medium-, and long-term goals • Model mistakes • Encourage your children to realize their own limitations • Discuss problems of asynchrony • Help children prioritize
Risk Evaders	• Adopt activities that are fun but not in an area of strength • Emphasize enjoyment over perfection • Upon completion of projects, notice areas of strength and areas for improvement • Share joys upon completion of projects rather than waiting for the teacher's evaluation • Encourage intellectual risk-taking
Controlling Image Managers	• Address frustrations from classmates through role-playing • Discuss competition using television, books, and other media • Help your children set personal goals, not comparative goals • Encourage risk-taking • Applaud your children's attempts and willingness to compete

TABLE 7, continued

Type of Perfectionist	Strategies to Use
Procrastinating Perfectionists	• Help your children find ways to relax standards during crunch times • Help your children make a plan for finishing long-term assignments • Check in regularly with your children to help maintain good work habits • Find nonstressful times to discuss time management with your children • Communicate regularly with your children's teachers • Use family projects as a way to model appropriate behaviors and healthy perfectionism

child's behavior has become unmanageable or if your child seems to be headed toward serious psychological or physical harm (such as depression, anxiety, or suicide), you pursue professional help from a psychologist, therapist, or licensed counselor. In fact, there is research evidence that cognitive behavioral therapy (CBT) is beneficial for those with unhealthy perfectionistic tendencies. This chapter is designed to give families who see unhealthy perfectionistic behaviors and tendencies in their children general activities and strategies to guide their children toward healthier behaviors and attitudes.

Crisis Moment Strategies

Some of the most trying times as a caregiver can be when your child reaches what we call a "crisis moment" in their unhealthy perfectionism. This is the moment when a child has a meltdown or tantrum or simply shuts down. It usually is precipitated by a stressful event (e.g., a project that is due, a forthcoming competition, or a major test). At that point, the child no longer is able to function in a rational or reasonable manner, and as the parent or adult you must find a solution that will be in the best interest of the child, while acknowledging the behaviors that contributed to the crisis moment.

Of course, the best way to deal with a crisis moment is to prevent one from occurring. However, as both parents and classroom teachers, we know that even the best and most resourceful caregivers find themselves in the midst of crisis moments periodically. The general strategies in the next section of this chapter will address techniques to employ when children are more calm and able to reflect and discuss their behaviors. When your child is in the middle of a meltdown, it is not the best time to try to develop strategies that may be helpful in the future. The key to these types of situations is to neutralize the strong emotions, cope with the immediate pressures (such as due dates, competitions, and tests), and focus your child's attention to the task at hand. **Preventative measures** can be taken later.

> *Your goal should be to prevent a crisis moment. However, when one occurs, you must use different strategies than you would to prevent such a moment.*

When your child is in the middle of an emotional time, it is difficult for them to think rationally or to understand the consequences of their previous actions. Thus, it is important for you to help your child calm down and cope with strong emotions in order to move forward in dealing with the task at hand. As a caregiver, you know your child the best and what steps to take to help your child calm down. Most children are soothed through personal contact, so a hug might be the best thing for the child facing stress. Soothing music, a quiet story, a walk around the block, deep breathing, or a short nap also may be helpful. If your child has been studying mindfulness, this is the perfect time to put these skills to use! If your child has been especially stressed or has stayed up late working on a project or studying, a short nap might really help your child improve their state of mind and be able to deal with the situation better. Try to avoid stimulating activities, such as television, which may work to increase your child's anxiety. The important part of this stage is to bring your child to a place where they can begin to tackle the project.

The next step is to help your child make a plan and cope with the immediate situation. For many Procrastinating Perfectionists, it is necessary to emphasize the importance of completing a task. You should highlight the accomplishment of finishing something you have started rather than focus on perfection or mistakes. On a tight deadline, it may be important to ignore some details of the project in order to relieve some stress. Help your child prioritize the details that should be addressed and others that might not be as important given the time limitations. In this situation, the important thing for you is to remain calm and avoid rushing your child. Although it may be difficult given the amount of stress that you are feeling, the additional emotions inevitably will create additional stress for your child. Also, although it may be tempting to "rescue" your child by doing some of the work for them, this does not set your child up for future success or teach them how to deal with these types of moments. Working with your child to make a realistic plan and address the situation, rather than just "solving the problem" for them, is important to how they handle future situations. It also lets them know that you believe that they have the skills, talent, and ability to handle these problems.

> *Resist the urge to "rescue" your child and to complete the work for them. Provide supports, but let your child do the work and accept the consequences for that work as well.*

Before beginning work, take a few minutes with your child to outline a plan for completing the assignment. This may mean eliminating some of the parts of the original assignment or ideas your child has for its completion, given the time limitations. It may be helpful to create a list of "must do" and "would like to do" items for the project and then decide what is realistic given the situation. This is a great tool to help your child express their vision for the project yet focus on what realistically can be accomplished. Let your child know that they can continue to improve on a project at a later time if they want, although it will be for personal satisfaction rather than for a grade or competition.

As your child begins work on the project, your role as a caregiver becomes crucial. Your child must be enabled to complete the work on their own. When a caregiver jumps in and completes the project or assignment, it reinforces the child's ideas about the need for perfection, elimination of all errors, and their own inadequacies. Instead, wait for your child to ask for specific help from you. Be careful to encourage your child to do tasks on their own, and help your child determine ways to complete the assignment on their own. This will help to foster the sense of accomplishment in your child's own work. However, you should always remember that if some element of the project or product requires a potentially dangerous situation, such as using hot glue or staple guns, or removing items from an oven, you should reasonably assist your child in performing these tasks. These are great moments to teach safety skills as well!

Throughout this process, it may become necessary to focus your child's attention to the immediate situation and work to be completed. It is easy for children to become distracted by their emotional states, especially when they are tied to their mounting stress surrounding the project, fear of failure, and unrealistic standards. When your child begins to become worried, gently redirect their attention back to the project. It may be necessary to take a few moments to help them identify what they are proud of in the project. Even if your child is unable to be satisfied with the entire project, they should be able to identify specific areas, such as the idea or particular details. It is easy for children to waste an enormous amount of time and energy on worry and stress. You should work to create a relaxing environment for your children to work in, free from external distractions and with needed materials at hand. You may need to give your child explicit permission not to be perfect. It also is important for you to offer your unconditional love and support to your child.

General Strategies

As mentioned previously, most families would like to prevent their child from reaching the point of frustration that leads to a meltdown. Although discussing a child's unhealthy perfectionistic behavior and tendencies is rarely successful during a moment of crisis, it can be quite beneficial during quiet times.

Although caregivers may have the tendency to lecture or address deeper issues when the child does not have control over their emotions, it usually is more productive to wait until times when the child is calmer, such as riding in the car or right before bed. Discussions with children about perfectionism and time management, along with purposeful family activities, can work to help change unhealthy perfectionism to healthy motivation and goals.

Discussions for You and Your Child

One topic that is especially important to discuss with children is the difference between healthy motivation and unhealthy perfectionism. A typical conversation might begin with discussing a general definition of perfectionism. This discussion should focus on specific behaviors. You and your child could identify both healthy and unhealthy behaviors. As the discussion continues about hypothetical situations, you can gently direct the conversation to situations from your child's own life. This can lead to a further discussion about healthy and unhealthy behaviors in your child's life. This might be a single discussion or a line of discussions that continues over a series of days or even weeks.

In addition, you might find teachable moments in your own life or in small examples in the life of your child to illustrate healthy motivation and goals or unhealthy perfectionism and unrealistic standards. Be careful about how you bring up examples of unhealthy perfectionism in your child's life. You do not want your child to feel judged or belittled. Bringing up examples in your own life and encouraging your child to think of examples from their life is one method of bringing these to light. If your child does not mention a particular behavior you would like to discuss, you might ask your child whether a particular behavior they exhibit seems unhealthy or healthy and discuss why. Remember that the purpose of the conversation is to help your child recognize these behaviors and how they help or hurt, not to lecture your child or make your child feel inferior or stressed about exhibiting perfectionistic behaviors.

Another line of discussion for caregivers and children is how to set goals. This discussion should cover setting long-, medium-, and short-term goals. These might include goals for the day, week, grading period, year, and far into the future. Be sure to emphasize not only the importance of goals, but also the steps to take to reach them. For example, if one goal is to become a doctor, then learning about biology and anatomy might be short-term goals to achieve that career. Emphasize activities and behaviors as steps to reach the goal rather than outcomes, such as "making good grades." Also, keep in mind that goals should include not just academic but also social, personal, and recreational objectives. One way to help your child understand how to set short- and long-term goals is to model these as a family. Family meetings are good ways to determine a family's goal for a year, month, or week. Perhaps you set a goal as a family to travel to an amusement park for vacation over the summer. Starting in the fall, you can set the vacation as a long-term goal and then demonstrate how you can set short-term goals to achieve it, such as saving your change and counting it each week to add to a bank account for the trip. Older children can help perform certain necessary short-term tasks along the way to a long-term goal, like researching vacation activities or making airline reservations. Projects around the home also are good examples of short- and long-term planning. Redecorating a child's bedroom, for instance, represents a long-term goal. Along the way, you and your child can plan short-term goals for weekend work, including making trips to the hardware store for paint, priming and painting walls, or picking out new comforters or curtains. After your child understands how to apply goal setting to everyday life, use that knowledge to help them make goals for schoolwork or activities of interest.

Along with goal setting, caregivers often need to discuss with their children time management and planning for long-term projects and goals. This is particularly important for Procrastinating Perfectionists who often delay work on a project until it reaches a crisis point. It also is important for perfectionists who spend an unhealthy amount of time on a particular project or schoolwork to the neglect of friendships, family relationships, or healthy habits, such as sleep or exercise. You should help your child prioritize important parts of their life and organize their schedule to spend time on each of them. In this case, it also is important for you to model these healthy habits. In modeling these habits, it may be helpful for you to look for teachable moments in the lives of famous people or characters in books, television, or movies. Children should realize that even the people they idolize make mistakes and have to make choices and prioritize. They also cannot excel at everything, but they should try many activities. You can use moments from your own life, admitting to your child when you make mistakes. Admitting such errors out loud and at the moment they occur can go a long way to showing your child that everyone makes mistakes in many situations.

> *Remember to help your child set short-, medium-, and long-term goals in academic, social, and personal areas.*

Through all of these discussions, you can help your child learn how to adapt their unhealthy perfectionistic behaviors and unrealistic standards to healthy motivation and goals. You can always be on the lookout for teachable moments that might spark a conversation.

Family Time Activities

One easy way to begin family activities is to find something that family members find fun but in which no one is particularly talented. This gives everyone a chance to let loose and have fun without the pressure of performing perfectly. It also will give children a safe place to fail or not be successful. In these activities, it is important that children have the chance not to be the winner in competitive situations. These activities might be physical, intellectual, or recreational, such as board games, playing Frisbee, singing karaoke, doing craft projects, or playing volleyball in the backyard.

Another family activity is to have regular celebrations of effort and process. Rather than celebrate on report card day, have a celebration at the end of the marking period *before* the report cards are sent home. This time should celebrate the hard work during the time period rather than the child's achievements. Other examples might be to celebrate the end of a large project or the practice leading up to a big competition. These celebrations do not need to be expensive; rather, they can be simple activities. Even a trip to a favorite local restaurant, ordering pizza, having game night at home, going to the park, or baking a special treat might be a way to celebrate a child's effort or process. Celebrating the achievement of goals for each member of the family (adults included) sets an atmosphere that treasures hard work and completion of tasks.

Many parenting resources and experts recommend family game nights as a way for families to connect and spend time together. For families dealing with unhealthy perfectionistic behaviors and tendencies, game nights can serve an additional purpose. Games can provide a safe place for children to practice both winning and losing. Especially if children have trouble dealing with losing in social situations with their peer group, game nights can provide a time for children to practice losing in a supportive environment. Other families may wish to avoid competitive games and focus on jigsaw puzzles, team games, or games that promote cooperation, such as Family Fluxx, the Ungame, Hoot Owl Hoot!, or Forbidden Island. (See Chapter 11 for a description of these and other cooperative games.) These types of games can promote effort and process over achievement.

Family activities, such as game nights and celebrations of effort, can provide ways for family members to enjoy each other while helping children avoid unhealthy perfectionistic tendencies and behaviors. Activities, along with discussion, can help caregivers and children work together to transition to healthy motivation and goals. These activities are a starting point for families, but creative caregivers and children can look for other ways to connect and help combat unhealthy perfectionism.

> *Children often learn their values from their caregivers, so be sure to show them that the process and improvements made are important, not just grades and winning.*

Homework

Few caregivers (or children) look forward to nightly homework assignments. However, this time can be a particular struggle for families dealing with unhealthy perfectionistic behaviors and tendencies. Structuring homework time to be most successful for children may help to ease the frustration and tension that often comes with it. These techniques will work for both long-term projects and short-term assignments.

The first step is to set up an environment that is conducive to studying. All children need a quiet place to complete their work, with ample space to write and adequate lighting. It also may be helpful to store school supplies and other necessities in the vicinity. This place should be free from distractions, such as the television and other family members playing or working. Especially for Procrastinating Perfectionists, an environment with such distractions tends to lead to many hours spent "on homework" with little of that time actually devoted to the homework. You child may enjoy and feel motivated to do projects when they have input into designing and setting up an ideal workspace.

In addition to creating the physical space to do homework, children also need a dedicated time each night to do homework. This need not be the exact same time each evening, as afterschool and extracurricular activities often prevent such a schedule, but you need to help your child schedule a time for homework each night. Write this dedicated homework time into your child's agenda or planner or on a family calendar. (For an example of planning a schedule, see the calendar in Chapter 4.)

During homework time, it is essential that you be available to support your child while they are working. This does not mean that you are overseeing the work or checking your child's answers. On the other hand, you should ensure that your child is able to ask you questions if they are unsure about an assignment or concept or need help. In some situations, it might be beneficial for your child to see you working on your own projects or reading a book at the same time they are expected to do so, setting the climate that intellectual challenges are acceptable and enjoyable. In other situations, however, this may be distracting to your child.

In addition, you should take great care not to complete your child's work for them or help without being asked. These behaviors can take away from your child's own sense of accomplishment in the process of completing work and emphasize the importance of the final product rather than the learning that occurs. Completing work for your child demonstrates a need for perfection and implies that your child cannot perform perfectly without you. Additionally, you should resist always checking your child's answers (but you can check for completion when necessary). Children need to understand that homework is an opportunity to practice what they are learning and that they do not have to be perfect on each assignment. You should work with your child's teacher to understand the homework policy, including how the teacher grades homework and whether your child receives feedback. Ideally, the focus is on practice and learning, so families should use returned homework to talk with their child about what was learned and if further practice is needed to master the concepts.

Most children need support from their families to plan and prioritize assignments. In less mature children, families will need to provide more support, and as the child grows and learns they can build toward more independence. These are the types of life skills that you, as a caregiver, can help to instill in your child and that will be beneficial for your child's future in high school, college, and the workplace. In the beginning, you may need to write a schedule with specific goals for each day with your child. Additionally, you may need to check in with your child each day to see how they are meeting these goals. As your child progresses, you should be able to take less of the responsibility for making the goals and check in with your child less often.

Many of the frustrations and conflicts that arise because of homework stem from miscommunication between the child and/or caregiver and the teacher. When families have good communication with educators, children benefit. At the beginning of the year, it is helpful for you, as a caregiver, to get information about the expectations for homework from each of your child's teachers. In particular, it is helpful to know how much time your child's teacher expects them to spend on homework each night. If your child seems to be experiencing stress concerning assignments, then it is appropriate for you to arrange an additional meeting with your child's teacher to clear up any miscommunication. Remember that the stress may be stemming from your child's internal desires for achievement rather than from expectations from the teacher. In addition, when there is an occasion to celebrate, be sure to communicate with the teacher. It is important to convey both negative and positive events. Using a homework agenda or planner is a useful tool for communication between families, educators, and child. If your child's school or teacher does not require a planner, you might consider purchasing one for your child and teaching them how to use it. In this planner, the child can record upcoming projects and tests so that they can prepare in advance, and families and educators can communicate with each other about successes or missing work.

During homework time, you can help your child by teaching them to accept less-than-perfect standards, especially given a reasonable amount of time. Although many children feel pressure to turn in assignments without flaws or mistakes, this expectation is unreasonable and will become increasingly difficult as the rigor of the curriculum increases. You can help your child realize the difference between ideal and reality by helping them to understand what expectations are realistic given the limitations of time, dexterity, and well-being. Furthermore, you should talk with your child about **formative assessments**, or the opportunity for them to practice what they are learning. In most cases, educators use homework as a time for students to practice what they have learned rather than to assess mastery.

> Remember that motivation and goals can be healthy!

Finally, you are an important influence in your child's life when it comes to prioritizing activities. Homework and long-term projects should never compromise your child's health. For example, a regular bedtime and proper amounts of sleep are vital for your child's health and should not be adjusted to finish homework. At these times, you may want to consider writing a note to your child's teacher explaining the situation without necessarily asking for more time or an exception. Children do need to see that they are not expected to be perfect; sometimes they cannot fit everything into their lives, but there are consequences for the choices they make. In addition, your child may need help prioritizing activities, such as spending time with family and friends, as well as devoting time to schoolwork. Healthy social relationships and a balance of fun and work are important for every person's life.

Final Thoughts

Everyone knows parenting is hard work, and parenting a child with unhealthy perfectionistic tendencies has its own unique challenges. However, having high expectations and motivation to succeed are assets to any child. Through the strategies in this chapter, your family can build toward developing healthy behaviors and attitudes that will lead your child to greater success.

CHAPTER 11

Resources for Children

Picture Books

Beautiful Oops! **by Barney Saltzberg, 2010, Workman**

This book illustrates how to incorporate mistakes, such as spills, smears, smudges, and tears, into artwork, making the "oops" into something beautiful.

The Book of Mistakes **by Corinna Luyken, 2017, Dial Books**

This book not only shows mistakes transformed into artwork, but also shares the artistic process that incorporates splotches, spots, and misshapen things.

The Dot **by Peter H. Reynolds, 2003, Candlewick**

Vashti does not want to draw because she believes she is not an artist. If she can't be perfect, why start a drawing? After procrastinating the entire art class, Vashti jabs at a blank sheet of paper, leaving one unremarkable dot. That dot is what gets her started, gets her unstuck, and teaches her about creativity.

The Girl Who Never Made Mistakes by Mark Pett and Gary Rubinstein, 2011, Sourcebooks

This book is about a girl who has never made mistakes and always wins the school's annual talent show. Then, one day she not only makes a mistake, but also makes it in front of everyone. How will she deal with it?

Ish by Peter H. Reynolds, 2004, Candlewick

Ramon loves to draw, but when his older brother makes a remark, Ramon finds himself struggling and avoiding taking the risk of not getting his drawing right. His little sister helps him overcome his fear of not getting things just right.

Mistakes That Worked: 40 Familiar Inventions & How They Came to Be by Charlotte Foltz Jones, 1994, Delacorte Press

Kids learn that mistakes and imperfections can lead to unusual inventions, including Coca-Cola, sandwiches, Silly Putty, potato chips, X-rays, and more. This book includes not only unusual tales, but also cartoons and amazing facts.

The Most Magnificent Thing by Ashley Spires, 2014, Kids Can Press

The little girl has a very grand vision of what she wants to accomplish. "She is going to make the most MAGNIFICENT thing!" She develops her vision and thinks it will be easy, but then trying to make her vision a reality is much more challenging than she thought.

Nobody's Perfect: A Story for Children About Perfectionism by Ellen Flanagan Burns, 2008, Magination Press

This story, written for ages 8–12, is about a young perfectionist, Sally Sanders. She worries about not measuring up and feeling like a failure. Through the sound advice of her mother and teacher, Sally learns how to overcome her perfectionism. This book provides an excellent way for children to see how their own behaviors may be connected to Sally's in the story.

Penelope Perfect: A Tale of Perfectionism Gone Wild
by Shannon Anderson, 2015, Free Spirit

It was one of those days when nothing goes according to plan. From oversleeping to wearing mismatched socks to earning her first-ever B, Penelope Perfect must deal with a very imperfect day.

A Perfectly Messed-Up Story by Patrick
McDonnell, 2014, Little, Brown

Louie is trying to share his story, but imperfections are constantly messing it up! He expresses his frustration as he tries to muddle through, and the messes just keep getting worse. In this fun read-aloud, kids experience Louie's emotions with him and can share in his lesson at the end of the book.

Stickley Makes a Mistake!: A Frog's Guide to Trying
Again by Brenda S. Miles, 2016, Magination Press

Stickley the frog makes mistakes and gets very frustrated, but his grandpa shares encouraging phrases and words to help motivate Stickley to keep trying.

Chapter Books

Be a Perfect Person in Just Three Days! by Stephen
Manes, 2018, Cadwallader & Stern

In this story written for ages 9–12, the main character, Milo, reads a book and follows steps to become perfect in just 3 days, including wearing a stalk of broccoli around his neck for a full day. In the end, he learns that being perfect is just not fun. (Note for educators: This is a great read-aloud during the first week or so of school.)

Beezus and Ramona by Beverly Cleary, 2020, HarperCollins

The first in the Ramona series, this book (originally written in 1955) features Ramona's older sister, Beezus, and a preschool Ramona, who always seems to be getting into trouble. Beezus has difficulties keeping up her "perfect" persona, while less-than-perfect Ramona seems to be getting the better end of the deal. This book provides many opportunities to discuss perfectionism with children.

***A Crooked Kind of Perfect* by Linda Urban,**
2007, Houghton Mifflin Harcourt
A 10-year-old girl named Zoe demonstrates resiliency when dreams and goals don't go as planned. Zoe, a budding musician, relies on the support of her unique family and friends and her own ingenuity to compete in a music competition. This book, filled with hope and humor, can provide role models for young perfectionists in grades 4–6.

***Cubed: The Puzzle of Us All* by Erno Rubik, 2020, Flatiron Books**
This nonfiction book is written by the inventor of the Rubik's Cube. He shares about lessons he has learned, including learning from mistakes and failures. He discusses curiosity, being a creator, and taking risks.

***Harry Potter* series by J. K. Rowling, Scholastic**
The popular books (and movies) about the young students at Hogwarts School of Witchcraft and Wizardry lend themselves well to a discussion of perfectionism in the character of Hermione. Hermione, an overachieving student, can serve as an example for other children who must overcome perfectionism. One particular quote from Chapter 6 of *Harry Potter and the Sorcerer's Stone* that embodies Hermione's perfectionism is: "Are you sure that's a real spell? . . . Well, it's not very good, is it? I've tried a few simple spells just for practice and it's all worked for me. Nobody in my family's magic at all, it was ever such a surprise when I got my letter, but I was ever so pleased. . . . I've learned all our course books by heart, of course. I just hope it will be enough." *Harry Potter and the Prisoner of Azkaban* specifically provides opportunities to think about and discuss time management and the need to prioritize. Hermione, like many children with perfectionistic tendencies, has many talents and wants to succeed in them all, so she uses a Time Turner to attend extra classes that take place at the same time. This provides an opportunity to talk about limitations, scheduling, prioritizing, and decisions.

***Izzy, Willy-Nilly* by Cynthia Voigt, 2005, Atheneum**
Izzy has a perfect life as a cheerleader and popular student, but that is shattered when she is in a car accident that results in the loss of her leg. Throughout the book, written for middle school students, Izzy must learn to cope with her new identity and less-than-perfect life. This book can provide another role model for students who are seeking the perfect image, and learn to appreciate the inner characteristics of a person.

Jaclyn Hyde by Annabeth Bondor-Stone and Connor White, 2019, HarperCollins

Although Jaclyn Hyde is *almost* perfect, she can't resist the lure of a batch of perfection potion. However, the potion turns her into Jackie, a goblin-like alter ego who will stop at nothing to ensure Jaclyn is perfect.

Millicent Min, Girl Genius by Lisa Yee, 2004, Scholastic

This book, written for grades 5–8, features Millie, an 11-year-old who has been accelerated into high school. Tired of being thought of as a genius, Millie uses her senior year to try to hide her abilities and have a more normal existence. However, when her new friends find out the truth, they feel betrayed and hurt. This book speaks about the importance of honesty, being true to yourself, and realizing your abilities.

The Mysterious Benedict Society by Trenton Lee Stewart, 2008, Little, Brown

Aimed at grades 5–9, this book is about a special group of gifted kids who band together to defeat the evil Mr. Curtain. Each of the characters has a unique personality and must work to overcome their fears throughout the adventure. This book provides role models for students to face their own fears.

Rules by Cynthia Lord, 2008, Scholastic

Written for upper elementary and middle school students, this chapter book is about a girl with a brother who has autism. Through her creation of "rules" for his behavior and a developing friendship with another boy with special needs, Catherine discovers deeper relationships. This book can help students redefine "normal" and develop role models.

Stanford Wong Flunks Big-Time by Lisa Yee, 2007, Scholastic

A companion book to *Millicent Min, Girl Genius*, this book tells the story of the sixth-grade boy who Millicent tutors. Faced with enormous pressure from his family to achieve and summer school, Stanford undergoes a change of heart. Written for grades 5–8, this book can provide an example for children who feel pressure to be perfect.

A Summer to Die by Lois Lowry, 2016, Houghton Mifflin Harcourt

Meg idolizes her big sister Molly, who she sees as being absolutely perfect and flawless in every way. When Molly gets leukemia, Meg has to come to terms with both her sister's illness and her own unique gifts—in this case, photography. This book, written for a middle school audience, can provide examples of how to appreciate your gifts while accepting faults.

The View From Saturday by E. L. Konigsburg, 1998, Atheneum
Recommended for ages 9–12, this chapter book describes a sixth-grade academic trivia team. Despite the diverse group of characters, students work together to contribute to the team effort. This story of friendship can provide an excellent example of healthy competition.

Note. For other book suggestions, please see Adderholdt-Elliott and Eller's (1989) article listed in Chapter 12 and in the References, as well as Hébert's (2020) *Understanding the Social and Emotional Lives of Gifted Students* (2nd ed.).

Self-Help Books

Bust Your Buts: Tips for Teens Who Procrastinate by Joanne Foster, 2017, Great Potential Press
This book includes hundreds of tricks to help procrastinators, whether they are the occasional procrastinator or consistently find themselves acting like Procrastinating Perfectionists. Using those tips, teens can use their time better and become more productive.

Perfectionism: What's Bad About Being Too Good (Rev. ed.) by Miriam Adderholdt and Jan Goldberg, 1999, Free Spirit
This book, a classic in perfectionism literature, is aimed primarily at preteen and teenage youth. Speaking directly to this audience, the authors provide advice and define terms for young perfectionists. Although some of the research that supports this book is somewhat dated, it provides valuable insights for young people.

***The Perfectionism Workbook for Teens: Activities to Help you Reduce
Anxiety and Get Things Done* by Ann Marie Dobosz, Instant Help**
This book is based on cognitive behavioral therapy (CBT) and gives
teens tools to develop self-compassion and mindfulness with the goal of
healthy skills and higher self-confidence.

***See You Later, Procrastinator! (Get It Done)* by Pamela
Espeland and Elizabeth Verdick, 2008, Free Spirit**
Part of a self-help series for kids, this illustrated nonfiction book provides tips and strategies to help kids stay on track and motivated to accomplish their goals. Using humor and full-color cartoons, this book gives procrastinators easy-to-implement strategies for changing their habits.

***The Survival Guide for Gifted Kids* by Judy
Galbraith, 2013, Free Spirit**
Covering a wide variety of social and emotional issues of gifted children, this book is written directly to children ages 10 and under. It contains
a chapter dealing with perfectionism and can provide support for gifted
children.

***What to Do When Good Enough Isn't Good Enough: The Real Deal
on Perfectionism* by Thomas S. Greenspon, 2007, Free Spirit**
Speaking directly to children, this book provides advice for young
perfectionists. Aimed at ages 9–12, the author provides instructions for
children on how to cope with perfectionism and change their negative
behaviors and thought patterns.

***What to Do When Mistakes Make You Quake: A Kid's
Guide to Accepting Imperfection* by Claire A. B. Freeland
and Jacqueline B. Toner, 2015, Magination Press**
This book is an interactive self-help book for children and their caregivers about coping with mistakes and the emotions that underlie the fear
of making mistakes. The strategies and techniques presented in the book
are based on cognitive-behavioral principles and are designed for kids who
are 6–12 years old.

***What to Do When You're Scared and Worried: A Guide
for Kids* by James J. Crist, 2004, Free Spirit**

As part of a self-help series for kids, this book provides support for children suffering from anxiety. Dealing with both normal fears and worries and more serious problems (such as anxiety disorder and obsessive-compulsive disorder), the friendly and light tone of the book will reassure children and give them practical strategies for coping with worries.

Games

Dinosaur Escape, Peaceable Kingdom

Dinosaur Escape is a cooperative game in which players have to use memory and logic and have some luck in order to escape to safety before the volcano blows. This game is great for younger players (manufacturer recommended for ages 4+).

Family Fluxx, Looney Labs

Kids may think they are about to win, when suddenly, a new card enters the picture, changing everything! In this card game, the rules constantly are being altered by the presence of new cards that can shift the gameplay dramatically. It's a great card game for promoting the idea of chance and the notion that sometimes going against the standard rules is really fun.

Forbidden Island, Forbidden Desert, and *Forbidden Sky,* Gamewright

These three cooperative strategy games are about survival and will require your team to talk with one other to strategize how to survive. The manufacturer's recommendation is ages 10+, but we have played them with younger gifted children. Forbidden Island is the least complex and involves capturing four sacred treasures before the island sinks. In Forbidden Desert, your team must survive a blowing sandstorm and scorching sun to recover pieces of a legendary flying machine that have been buried in the ruins of an ancient desert city. The most complex of the three games, Forbidden Sky involves constructing a real electrical circuit as your team attempts to launch a rocket before being struck by lightning or blown off the mysterious platform floating in a storm.

Hoot Owl Hoot!, Peaceable Kingdom

In this cooperative game, players help the owls try to fly back to their nest before sunrise. There are instructions to decrease or increase the difficulty as players develop strategies to help the owls. This game is great for younger players (manufacturer recommended for ages 4+).

Mermaid Island, Peaceable Kingdom

With a little strategy and lots of luck, players work together in this cooperative game to help the mermaids swim to Mermaid Island before the sea witch gets there. This game is great for younger players (manufacturer recommended for ages 5+). *Note.* Peaceable Kingdom makes other cooperative games for young children. We recommend checking them out for fun family games.

Outfoxed!, Gamewright

Outfoxed! is a cooperative whodunit game that requires deduction and some luck. Players work together to rule out suspects, trying to figure out which fox stole Mrs. Plumpert's prized pot pie before the fox gets away with it (manufacturer recommended for ages 5+).

Pandemic, Z-Man Games

For older elementary school kids, adolescents, and adults (manufacturer recommended ages of 8+), Pandemic offers a challenging cooperative board game that puts players in the roles of members of a disease-fighting team. Players must work together to stop the outbreak of four diseases that threaten the world and discover the cures to the diseases.

The Sleeping Grump, Family Pastimes

In this imaginative board game, players work together to climb the beanstalk without waking the sleeping grump. Players share their treasures and together win the game when everyone, including the grump, has their share. This game emphasizes cooperative work.

The Ungame, TaliCor

The Ungame is a noncompetitive game that fosters self-expression and communication. Expansion packs can be purchased for families, teens, and children. As players move around the board, questions ask players to reflect on things such as, "What are the most important things in your life?" and "What do you think life will be like in 100 years?"

CHAPTER 12

Resources for Adults

Books and Articles for Caregivers and Educators

"Counseling Students Who Are Gifted Through Bibliotherapy" by Miriam Adderholdt-Elliott and Suzanne Eller, 1989, *Teaching Exceptional Children*, 22(1), 26–31. https://doi.org/10.1177/004005998902200106

The authors of this article present a rationale for using bibliotherapy, particularly with students who are gifted but also with children of all ability levels, and then explain the process of using bibliotherapy in the classroom. They provide an example using a unit on perfectionism with high school students and with elementary and middle school students. This article provides details about several fiction and nonfiction books that could be used for bibliotherapy on perfectionism, including *The Autobiography of Benjamin Franklin* by Benjamin Franklin, *Tales for the Perfect Child* by Florence Parry Heide, *Fables* by Arnold Lobel, and *Where Do You Think You're Going, Christopher Columbus?* by Jean Fritz.

***Everyone Wins: Cooperative Games and Activities* by Josette Luvmour and Sambhava Luvmour, 2007, New Society Publishers**

This book provides instructions for many cooperative games appropriate for a variety of age and activity levels. These games emphasize cooperation and communication rather than competitiveness. These games can help families and children discover the fun of participation and process rather than focus on the final outcome.

"A 'Perfect' Case Study: Perfectionism in Academically Talented Fourth Graders" by Jill L. Adelson, 2007, *Gifted Child Today*, *30*(4), 14–20. https://doi.org/10.4219/gct-2007-490

This article, which *Letting Go of Perfect* (2nd ed.) was based on, provides case studies of perfectionism among gifted students. It provides information and background on perfectionism among elementary students.

***Social, Emotional, and Psychosocial Development of Gifted and Talented Individuals* by Anne N. Rinn, 2020, Prufrock Press**

This book provides research-based information on the social, emotional, and psychosocial development of gifted and talented children. It helps educators, families, and practitioners distinguish between facts and myths within the field of gifted education. The chapter on perfectionism, along with others, provides a foundation of what is known in the field about topics.

***Some of My Best Friends Are Books: Guiding Gifted Readers* (3rd ed.) by Judith Wynn Halsted, 2009, Great Potential Press**

This book provides an explanation of how to use bibliotherapy with gifted children and recommendations for many of the issues that face gifted children, including perfectionism. Each list of recommendations is divided into age-appropriate selections and includes a synopsis of the book.

Books for Families

***The Art of Learning: An Inner Journey to Optimal Performance* by Josh Waitzkin, 2008, Free Press**
The beginning of this book, written by the chess prodigy that the film *Searching for Bobby Fischer* was based on, describes how one family was able to allow a very talented boy to avoid perfectionism and live a relatively normal childhood while still developing his talents. The insights that he provides throughout the book can serve as a model to many families in the balance of healthy and unhealthy perfectionism.

***The Good Enough Child: How to Have an Imperfect Family and Be Perfectly Satisfied* by Brad E. Sachs, 2001, HarperCollins**
This book provides advice for caregivers on how to accept your children as they come, without unrealistic expectations. The path of parenting is unpredictable, and this book provides a guide for negotiating unexpected twists and turns.

***Success Strategies for Parenting Gifted Kids: Expert Advice From the National Association for Gifted Children* edited by Kathleen Nilles, Jennifer L. Jolly, Tracy Ford Inman, and Joan Franklin Smutny, 2019, Prufrock Press**
This collection of articles from the National Association for Gifted Children's publication *Parenting for High Potential* provides background from leading experts on a variety of parenting topics for gifted children. This resource for families covers a broad expanse of topics, including social and emotional development, perfectionism, anxiety, and helping families advocate within school settings.

***Understanding Your Gifted Child From the Inside Out: A Guide to the Social and Emotional Lives of Gifted Kids* by James R. Delisle, 2018, Prufrock Press**
This book provides down-to-earth advice for parents of gifted children. Putting forth tips for caregivers, reflecting the author's experience with gifted children, the book focuses on enjoying life with your child and focusing on the moment. Dr. Delisle is well known for his work with gifted children and families, and this book provides perspectives and reintroduces joy to parenting.

Books for Educators

Mindfulness in the Classroom: Strategies for Promoting Concentration, Compassion, and Calm **by Thomas Armstrong, 2019, ASCD**

This book provides a nice overview and specific techniques for educators wishing to incorporate mindfulness techniques into their classroom and practice more self-care for themselves.

The Morning Meeting Book **(3rd ed.) by Roxann Kriete and Carol Davis, 2014, Northeast Foundation for Children**

The morning meeting is a way for educators to foster a sense of community among their students and provide time for discussing such issues as perfectionism. This book provides guidelines and examples for group activities.

Books for Adult Perfectionists

The CBT Workbook for Perfectionism: Evidence-Based Skills to Help You Let Go of Self-Criticism, Build Self-Esteem, and Find Balance **by Sharon Martin, 2019, New Harbinger Publications**

This interactive workbook uses a foundation of cognitive behavioral therapy to help adults change their habits of mind and break the cycle of perfectionistic thinking. This book provides concrete self-help strategies to living a healthier life.

The Gifts of Imperfection: Let Go of Who You Think You're Supposed to Be and Embrace Who You Are **by Brené Brown, 2010, Hazeldon Publishing**

A national bestseller, this book has inspired millions to change the ways in which they think about their lives. Brown is able to use storytelling to help the reader change perspectives of self-doubt and perfectionistic thought toward acceptance and self-fulfillment.

*When Perfect Isn't Good Enough: Strategies for Coping
With Perfectionism* **by Martin M. Anthony and Richard
P. Swinson, 2009, New Harbinger Publications**
This book provides adults with strategies to overcome unhealthy perfectionism. When perfectionistic tendencies prevent you from achieving to your highest potential, this book can provide the background information and effective strategies for coping.

Web Resources About Mindfulness

"11 Ways to Teach Mindfulness to Kids" by Amy Morin
https://www.verywellfamily.com/ways-to-teach-mindfulness-to-kids-41 34344
This article provides concrete exercises for teaching preschoolers to teenagers mindfulness skills.

**"25 Fun Mindfulness Activities for Children
and Teens" by Courtney E. Ackerman**
https://positivepsychology.com/mindfulness-for-children-kids-activities
After reviewing some of the research on mindfulness, this article provides mindfulness activities and exercises; tips for teaching mindfulness to children and teenagers; recommendations for mindfulness games, YouTube videos, and apps; recommendations for mindfulness training classes for children with anxiety; videos for teaching mindfulness in schools; and more.

"Guided Meditation for Children" by Annaka Harris
https://annakaharris.com/mindfulness-for-children
Annaka Harris provides free recordings of her guided meditations. Although intended for ages 6–10, they can be used by older children, teens, and beginner-level adults.

**"How to Practice Mindfulness With Children—
The Essential Guide" by Chris Bergstrom**
https://blissfulkids.com/how-to-practice-mindfulness-with-children-the-essential-guide
This article includes age-based tips, recommendations for introducing mindfulness to your child, tips for first steps, mindfulness activities and techniques, and information about mindful parenting.

"Mindfulness for Children" by David Gelles
https://www.nytimes.com/guides/well/mindfulness-for-children
This article provides information for adults about mindfulness for children. With a section on each age group from infants to teenagers, it provides developmentally appropriate information about children and suggestions for mindfulness.

**"Mindfulness in Education: 31+ Ways of Teaching
Mindfulness in Schools" by Courtney E. Ackerman**
https://positivepsychology.com/mindfulness-education
After reviewing some of the research on mindfulness, this article describes what a mindfulness curriculum includes and provides mindfulness resources and activities. It also provides several resources, including recommended books and TED Talks.

**"Mindfulness in Education Research Highlights"
by the Greater Good Science Center**
https://greatergood.berkeley.edu/images/uploads/Mindfulness_in_Education_Research_Highlights.pdf
This document provides an annotated bibliography of research on mindfulness and students, mindfulness and educators, and mindfulness and administrators.

"Resources on Mindfulness in Education" by Edutopia
https://www.edutopia.org/article/mindfulness-resources
This article includes an annotated list of resources about mindfulness, including links to learn about potential benefits of mindfulness for learning; ways to introduce mindfulness in the classroom, implement school-wide and afterschool mindfulness programs, and foster educator wellness and effectiveness through mindfulness; and resources and downloads

from schools. Also included are links to posts on other topics, such as how to translate mindfulness to distance learning.

Resources for Families in Crisis

APA Psychologist Locator
https://locator.apa.org
This resource from the American Psychological Association helps parents and families locate mental health professionals, by specialty, in their local areas.

National Institute of Mental Health: Children and Mental Health
https://www.nimh.nih.gov/health/publications/children-and-mental-health/index.shtml
This webpage provides a guide for parents and families on mental health for children, including resources and guidelines.

National Suicide Prevention Lifeline, 1-800-273-8255
https://suicidepreventionlifeline.org
This national network of local crisis centers provides emotional support for people and families experiencing suicidal crises or emotional distress 24 hours a day, 7 days a week.

Books on Anxiety and Stress

Anxiety-Free Kids: An Interactive Guide for Parents and Children **(2nd ed.) by Bonnie Zucker, 2017, Prufrock Press**
This book offers advice and strategies to help parents of children who are experiencing anxiety. It includes both a reader-friendly section for parents and a workbook for children in one volume. This guide emphasizes solutions for children and parents and involves children in the self-help process.

Helping Your Anxious Child: A Step-by-Step Guide for Parents
**by Ronald M. Rapee, Ann Wignall, Susan H. Spence, Vanessa
Cobham, and Heidi Lyneham, 2008, New Harbinger Publications**
This book is designed for parents who have children who are experiencing extreme anxiety or have been diagnosed with anxiety disorders. It provides practical strategies and advice for parents that are based on sound research.

The Relaxation and Stress Reduction Workbook **(7th
ed.) by Martha Davis, Elizabeth Robbins Eshelman, and
Matthew McKay, 2019, New Harbinger Publications**
This book provides instruction in the latest research-based techniques for reducing stress and anxiety among children. These powerful relaxation techniques include progressive relaxation, visualization, and mindfulness and acceptance therapy.

Books on Eating Disorders

*8 Keys to Recovery From an Eating Disorder: Effective Strategies
From Therapeutic Practice and Personal Experience* **by
Carolyn Costin and Gwen Schubert Grabb, 2011, Norton**
This book provides a unique perspective to overcoming eating disorders, written by two therapists who have suffered from these disorders in the past. The interweaving of their narratives, along with the strategies for success and the insights of mental health professionals, provides an empathetic and supportive resource.

*By Their Side: A Resource for Caretakers and Loved Ones Facing
an Eating Disorder* **by Lara Lyn Bell, 2019, Brown Books**
This guide, written specifically for families and caretakers, provides supportive communication strategies to help loved ones with eating disorders. Providing both practical strategies and personal stories from those with experiences, this book gives insights and concrete steps to take.

Glossary

Academic Achiever: One type of perfectionist who holds unrealistically high expectations for their performance in academic pursuits. This kind of perfectionist focuses on the final grade and mistakes made.

Academically gifted children: Children who achieve highly in academic domains or are especially talented in school-related areas, such as mathematics or verbal skills.

Aggravated Accuracy Assessor: One type of perfectionist who focuses on making every detail perfect. They may choose to redo the same work over and over to try to make it more like their mind's ideal, may look frantically for ways to "fix" the work or find the necessary materials, or may become disappointed and give up trying.

Anorexia: A serious eating disorder in which a person does not eat or eats very little. Many people suffering from anorexia display clinical perfectionism.

Anxiety disorders: Disabling conditions in which a person is overcome by anxiety, including stress, phobias, or fears; many people with anxiety disorders also exhibit clinical perfectionism.

Assessment: Any type of evaluation that an educator or other professional might give to a student. This may include informal observations, standardized tests, or other forms of classroom grading.

Asynchronous development: A common feature of the development of children, in which one area of a child's development proceeds at a more rapid pace than another. For example, gifted children's minds may develop faster than their bodies, especially when physical skills are involved, such as in art, music, and sports.

Attention Deficit/Hyperactivity Disorder (ADHD): A disorder of executive functioning that can exhibit itself through inattention, hyperactivity, or both. A diagnosis of ADHD should be made through a psychologist, pediatrician, or other mental health professional.

Authoritarian parenting: A parenting style characterized by high expectations with low levels of nurturing or support.

Authoritative parenting: A parenting style characterized by supportive and nurturing parents who hold children to high standards.

Bibliotherapy: A type of therapy commonly used with children, in which books are used to address common social or emotional issues.

Buffers: Time that is built into a time management plan for when something does not go as planned or does not meet expectations and standards. Buffers can help children with perfectionism because when mistakes are made, they do not feel that they have failed already and that there is no need to continue.

Bulimia: A serious eating disorder in which a person enters a cycle of binging and purging food. People suffering from bulimia often exhibit clinical perfectionism.

Clinical perfectionism: Perfectionism that needs professional intervention, such as therapy, in-patient treatment, or further diagnoses.

Cognitive behavioral therapy (CBT): A type of therapy that focuses on adjusting the negative thought patterns, assumptions, beliefs, evaluations, and behaviors of people into more positive and healthy outcomes. This therapy has been shown to reduce perfectionism as well as depression and anxiety.

Concrete goals: Goals that have tangible and measurable outcomes. For instance, "learning five more multiplication facts this week" is a concrete goal, whereas "improving my multiplication skills" is not.

Controlling Image Manager: A type of perfectionist who wants others to regard them as perfect. If they are afraid that they will be unable to meet their own or others' expectations in competitive situations, they may choose to eliminate themselves from competition intentionally or create a face-saving situation, saying that they could have been perfect.

Crisis moments: The period when unhealthy perfectionism is most difficult for families, children, and educators to cope with. It often occurs when a child is throwing a tantrum, has completely shut down, or is overwhelmed by the current task.

Curriculum compacting: A technique commonly used with advanced learners, in which educators give a diagnostic assessment to assess what portions of an upcoming unit of study a student has already mastered and then replace material the student already has mastered with a more appropriate learning activity.

Depression: A serious condition in which a person feels sad or down for an extended period of time and that interferes with daily life and normal functioning or causes pain. People with depression often show higher levels of clinical perfectionism.

Diagnostic assessment or test: A type of assessment used at the beginning of a course of study to document the level of mastery a student has achieved prior to beginning instruction. This also is referred to as preassessment or pretesting.

Dichotomous thinking: The tendency to view events in life as either bad or good, with little or no gray area in between. This type of thinking often is associated with perfectionism.

Domain-specific perfectionism: Perfectionism that is displayed in one area of life, such as academics, but not in others.

Eating disorders: Serious conditions in which a person persists in unhealthy eating habits, such as anorexia or bulimia. People with eating disorders often exhibit clinical perfectionism.

Evaluative concerns perfectionism: A type of perfectionism that focuses on mistakes and self-criticism.

Extrinsic rewards: Rewards for achievement that exist outside of a person; for example, praise from an educator, stickers, or candy.

Fear of failure: One sign of perfectionism; an intense fear of failure can prevent some people from trying new activities, taking risks, or attempting challenges.

Flawed protagonist: The lead character in a story, movie, or book who makes mistakes, has character defects, or displays imperfections in other ways.

Formal assessments: Evaluations given by educators or other professionals that document learning or mastery. Formal assessments tend to be written, such as a standardized test or a unit test developed by the educator. They also may take the form of a rubric to document more subjective evaluations.

Formative assessments: Assessments that are typically given at the beginning or during of a unit of study to evaluate student mastery of concepts, skills, or knowledge so that the educator can assess students' current knowledge and skills and plan further instruction and learning experiences. Diagnostic assessments are one type of formative assessment.

Goal setting: The process of making goals and developing a plan for reaching those goals. This is a common way to help people with perfectionism develop healthier habits.

Goals: Objectives that one sets in hopes of reaching them within a set period of time.

Healthy motivation: Sometimes called adaptive or healthy perfectionism; represents the characteristics that are positive for students, including gaining a sense of pride from achievements and improvement and a drive for success.

Imposter syndrome: Common to some types of unhealthy perfectionism, it occurs when a person believes that other people's confidence in them is unwarranted. Those who experience imposter syndrome often have an intense fear of failure and need to mask their mistakes for fear of "discovery."

Independent study projects: One way that educators adapt the curriculum for advanced learners; students are allowed to study a topic of their own interest and develop a project to demonstrate their learning. Educators may choose to have students create and sign a contract describing the work they will do and how it will be assessed or evaluated.

Informal assessments: Evaluations that rely primarily on observation and less documented forms of evidence of student mastery or growth. Common informal assessments include anecdotal records, mind maps, or class discussions.

Instruments: Tests, assessments, or evaluation procedures that are used to diagnose, evaluate, or document various psychological constructs.

Intermediate goals: Goals that are set for an intermediate amount of time, usually between a few weeks and a few months. These also are referred to as medium-term goals.

Internal dialogue: A person's inner voice, usually a reflection of conscious thoughts.

Internal motivation: Motivation to accomplish tasks that comes from inside of a person; for example, internal motivation often comes from a drive to succeed or a love of learning.

Intrinsic motivation: See *Internal motivation.*

Intrinsic rewards: Rewards that come from within a person. For example, learning a new concept is described as the "joy of discovery."

Last-minute meltdown: When a child has not begun, much less finished, a major project the night before, or very close to, the due date and panics. This often occurs with Procrastinating Perfectionists.

Learning goals: Measurable goals for a student's learning, or mastery of content within the school curriculum.

Long-term goals: Goals that are set for a long period of time, typically between 1 and 5 years.

Medium-term goal: See *Intermediate goal.*

Metacognition: A tool for teaching in which students are instructed to think or reflect on their own thinking processes.

Mind map: A type of graphic organizer that allows students to record and organize their knowledge about a concept or topic. Mind maps consist of a main topic with branching subtopics and facts coming from the center.

Mixed-type perfectionism: A type of perfectionism that combines both evaluative concerns and personal standards.

Morning meeting: Typically a 10–15-minute period in which educators and students greet one another and do an activity or discuss an issue together. This time helps establish community and allows both the educator and students to address issues in a safe place rather than having these issues impact the entire day.

Motivation: The drive or force that propels a person to behave in a certain way, either desirable or undesirable.

Nonperfectionism: When a person does not appear to exhibit perfectionistic tendencies or behaviors.

Observational techniques: Strategies and protocols used in research and educational settings that rely primarily on observations made by educators or evaluators. These observations may be informal, such as the recording of anecdotes, or formal, such as the use of observation instruments.

Off-peak times: Times when your child is in a calm state, which may be ideal for discussing the effects of perfectionistic behaviors and tendencies.

Other-oriented perfectionism: When a child holds other people to high standards of perfection.

Overextended: A condition that is common among modern children, in which they are overly committed to extracurricular activities.

Parenting style: The way in which parents relate to their children. Parenting styles include authoritarian, authoritative (democratic), and passive.

Perfectionism: Refers to setting unreasonably high expectations of oneself, including an intolerance of mistakes.

Perfectionistic behaviors: Behaviors that a person exhibits that are tied to perfectionism, usually interpreted as unhealthy behaviors.

Perfectionistic tendencies: The inclination to engage in perfectionistic behaviors.

Performance goals: Goals that are tied directly to a person's measurable behaviors; goals related to one's own performance, such as improving by a measurable amount.

Permissive parenting: Parenting style in which parents view their children as equals and the children have few responsibilities.

Personal goals: Goals that are focused on what the child wants to improve, master, and enjoy, rather than on competition, like winning a competition or sport.

Personal standards perfectionism: A type of perfectionism that focuses on setting high standards and goals.

Pie chart: A graph that divides the whole into proportional parts using a circle. This type of organizer especially is helpful in aiding children to see how to prioritize their time.

Play therapy: Therapy that employs an interpersonal environment to evaluate and modify a child's behavior and cognitions. Popular strategies in play therapy include helping the child identify negative themes within their play, providing ways for the child to cope with mistakes and criticism, expanding the child's choices for play materials, helping the child cope with anxiety, and helping the child develop a greater tolerance for mistakes.

Psychological distress: Emotional or behavioral issues that prevent a person from normal functioning. Psychological distress sometimes is associated with unhealthy perfectionism.

Preventative measures: Steps taken to avoid unhealthy outcomes before they happen.

Prioritizing: The process of deciding to give certain tasks and activities more time and attention than other tasks or activities. This can help people who exhibit some types of perfectionistic tendencies to gain a healthier balance of activities.

Processing disorders: Disorders that disrupt the way in which the brain interprets and uses sensory information (such as auditory or visual). These disorders can create problems with academic and social functioning.

Problem-solving strategies: Techniques that educators and students use to solve problems, either in real-life or as part of the curriculum, such as word problems in mathematics class.

Procrastinating Perfectionist: One type of perfectionist who tends to plan an extensive project but then fails to start it for fear of their inability to achieve their perfect vision.

Procrastination: Putting off beginning activities or tasks until later, sometimes as a result of perfectionism and a fear of not meeting high expectations.

Realistic goals: Goals that can be obtained by a person; they may be based on high expectations but still are manageable given limitations of resources and time.

Risk Evader: A type of perfectionist who has a fear of failure to achieve their standards and ideals so they choose not to attempt the task.

Rumination: A fixation on interactions and events in the past, or reviewing past events over and over again in one's mind.

Scientific techniques: Strategies used in research settings utilizing measured outcomes, reliable instruments, and the scientific method.

Self-criticism: The tendency for some people to critique their own behavior in an overly negative way.

Self-esteem: How a person feels about themself in a global way; it most often is associated with an overall sense of self.

Self-oriented perfectionism: Perfectionism that occurs when a person feels the internal drive for high expectations.

Short-term goals: Goals that are set for a short period of time, usually between 1 and 3 weeks.

Socially prescribed perfectionism: A type of perfectionism when children believe that other people hold them to extremely high standards and are critical of their mistakes.

Subtasks: Smaller tasks that are part of a larger goal. By breaking down large tasks into smaller subtasks with concrete deadlines, students may be able to avoid procrastination and may gain a better sense of accomplishment and satisfaction with progress.

Suicide: A serious outcome of psychological distress in which a person takes their own life. Clinical perfectionism is associated with a higher risk for suicide.

Summative assessments: Assessments given by educators, researchers, or other professionals at the conclusion of a unit of study. Summative assessments measure the level of mastery of content by students.

Teachable moments: Moments that caregivers, educators, or other adults can use to illustrate a particular lesson or concept. These typically are spontaneous events that occur naturally within the course of the day of which the adult takes advantage to address or teach a particular concept.

Unrealistic goal: A goal that is unattainable given the limitations of resources, time, or ability. Unhealthy perfectionists often hold unrealistic goals for their own performance.

Videotherapy: A type of therapy commonly used with children, in which movies are used to address common social or emotional issues.

Well-balanced life: When children have a balance of healthy habits, including proper sleep, exercise, and eating habits, along with academic, extracurricular, social, and recreational time in their lives. This balance may vary from child to child but includes downtime along with other objectives.

WIMI (Why I Missed It): A strategy used by educators to allow students time for reflection and to ensure understanding of concepts covered on an assessment or practice work. See Figure 13 (p. 110) for an example.

References

Ablard, K. E., & Parker, W. D. (1997). Parents' achievement goals and perfectionism in their academically talented children. *Journal of Youth and Adolescence, 26*(6), 651–667. https://doi.org/10.1023/A:1022392524554

Adderholdt, M., & Goldberg, J. (1999). *Perfectionism: What's bad about being too good?* (Rev. ed). Free Spirit.

Adderholdt-Elliott, M., & Eller, S. (1989). Counseling students who are gifted through bibliotherapy. *Teaching Exceptional Children, 22*(1), 26–31. https://doi.org/10.1177/004005998902200106

Adelson, J. L. (2007). A "perfect" case study: Perfectionism in academically talented fourth graders. *Gifted Child Today, 30*(4), 14–20. https://doi.org/10.4219/gct-2007-490

Aldea, M. A. (2007). *Brief, online interventions for perfectionists* [Doctoral dissertation, University of Florida]. University of Florida Digital Collections. https://ufdcimages.uflib.ufl.edu/uf/e0/02/11/10/00001/aldea_m.pdf

Appleton, P. R., Hall, H. K., & Hill, A. P. (2010). Family patterns of perfectionism: An examination of elite junior athletes and their parents. *Psychology of Sport and Exercise, 11*(5), 363–371. https://doi.org/10.1016/j.psychsport.2010.04.005

Arpin-Cribbie, C. A., & Cribbie, R. A. (2007). Psychological correlates of fatigue: Examining depression, perfectionism, and automatic negative thoughts. *Personality and Individual Differences, 43*(6), 1310–1320. https://doi.org/10.1016/j.paid.2007.03.020

Arpin-Cribbie, C. A., Irvine, J., Ritvo, P., Cribbie, R. A., Flett, G. L., & Hewitt, P. L. (2008). Perfectionism and psychological distress: A modeling approach to understanding their therapeutic relationship. *Journal of Rational-Emotive & Cognitive-Behavior Therapy, 26*(3), 151–167. https://doi.org/10.1007/s10942-007-0065-2

Ashby, J. S., Kottman, T., & Martin, J. L. (2004). Play therapy with young perfectionists. *International Journal of Play Therapy, 13*(1), 35–55. https://doi.org/10.1037/h0088884

Beck, A. R., Verticchio, H., Seeman, S., Milliken, E., & Schaab, H. (2017). A mindfulness practice for CSD undergraduate and SLP graduate students: Effects on stress, self-compassion and perfectionism. *American Journal of Speech-Language Pathology, 26*(3), 893–907. https://doi.org/10.1044/2017_AJSLP-16-0172

Bardone-Cone, A. M. (2007). Self-oriented and socially prescribed perfectionism dimensions and their associations with disordered eating. *Behaviour Research and Therapy, 45*(8), 1977–1986. https://doi.org/10.1016/j.brat.2006.10.004

Biran, M. W., & Reese, C. (2007). Parental influences on social anxiety: The sources of perfectionism. *Journal of the American Psychoanalytic Association, 55*(1), 282–285. https://doi.org/10.1177/00030651070550010108

Blankstein, K. R., Lumley, C. H., & Crawford, A. (2007). Perfectionism, hopelessness, and suicide ideation: Revisions to diathesis-stress and specific vulnerability models. *Journal of Rational-Emotive & Cognitive-Behavior Therapy, 25*(4), 279–319. https://doi.org/10.1007/s10942-007-0053-6

Boergers, J., Spirito, A., & Donaldson, D. (1998). Reasons for adolescent suicide attempts: Associations with psychological functioning. *Journal of the American Academy of Child & Adolescent Psychiatry, 37*(12), 1287–1293. https://doi.org/10.1097/00004583-199812000-00012

Boisseau, C. L., Thompson-Brenner, H., Pratt, E. M., Farchione, T. J., & Barlow, D. H. (2013). The relationship between decision-making and perfectionism in obsessive-compulsive disorder and eating disorders. *Journal of Behavior Therapy and Experimental Psychiatry, 44*(3), 316–321. https://doi.org/10.1016/j.jbtep.2013.01.006

Boone, L., Soenens, B., Mouratidis, A., Vansteenkiste, M., Verstuyf, J., & Braet, C. (2012). Daily fluctuations in perfectionism dimensions and their relation to eating disorder symptoms. *Journal of Research in Personality, 46*(6), 678–687. https://doi.org/10.1016/j.jrp.2012.08.001

Burgess, A. M., Frost, R. O., & DiBartolo, P. M. (2016). Development and validation of the Frost Multidimensional Perfectionism Scale–Brief. *Journal of Psychoeducational Assessment, 34*(7), 620–633. https://doi.org/10.1177/0734282916651359

Callard-Szulgit, R. (2003). *Perfectionism and gifted children.* Scarecrow Education.

Castro-Fornieles, J., Gual, P., Lahortiga, F., Gila, A., Casulá, V., Fuhrmann, C., Imirizaldu, M., Saura, B., Martínez, E., & Toro, J. (2007). Self-oriented perfectionism in eating disorders. *International Journal of Eating Disorders, 40*(6), 562–568. https://doi.org/10.1002/eat.20393

Chang, E. C. (2013). Perfectionism and loneliness as predictors of depressive and anxious symptoms in Asian and European Americans: Do self-construal schemas also matter? *Cognitive Therapy and Research, 37*(6), 1179–1188. https://doi.org/10.1007/s10608-013-9549-9

Chang, E. C., Ivezaj, V., Downey, C. A., Kashima, Y., & Morady, A. R. (2008). Complexities of measuring perfectionism: Three popular perfectionism measures and their relations with eating disturbances and health behaviors in a female college student sample. *Eating Behaviors, 9*(1), 102–110. https://doi.org/10.1016/j.eatbeh.2007.06.003

Chang, E. C., Zumberg, K. M., Sanna, L. J., Girz, L. P., Kade, A. M., Shair, S. R., Hermann, N. B., & Srivastava, K. (2007). Relationship between perfectionism and domains of worry in a college student population: Considering the role of BIS/BAS motives. *Personality and Individual Differences, 43*(4), 925–936. https://doi.org/10.1016/j.paid.2007.02.026

Cook, L. C., & Kearney, C. A. (2009). Parent and youth perfectionism and internalizing psychopathology. *Personality and Individual Differences, 46*(3), 325–330. https://doi.org/10.1016/j.paid.2008.10.029

Cook, L. C., & Kearney, C. A. (2014). Parent perfectionism and psychopathology symptoms and child perfectionism. *Personality and Individual Differences, 70*, 1–6. https://doi.org/10.1016/j.paid.2014.06.020

Craddock, A. E., Church, W., & Sands, A. (2009). Family of origin characteristics as predictors of perfectionism. *Australian Journal of Psychology, 61*(3), 136–144. https://doi.org/10.1080/00049530802239326

Curran, T., & Hill, A. P. (2019). Perfectionism is increasing over time: A meta-analysis of birth cohort differences from 1989 to 2016. *Psychological Bulletin, 145*(4), 410. https://doi.org/10.1037/bul0000138

Daigneault, S. D. (1999). Narrative means to Adlerian ends: An illustrated comparison of narrative therapy and Adlerian play therapy. *Journal of Individual Psychology, 55*(3), 298–315.

Damian, L. E., Stoeber, J., Negru, O., & Baban, A. (2014). Positive and negative affect in adolescents: An Investigation of the 2 x 2 model of perfectionism. *Cognition, Brain, Behavior, 18*(1), 1–16.

DeKryger, N. A. (2005). *Childhood perfectionism: Measurement, phenomenology, and development* (Publication No. 3208805) [Doctoral Dissertation, University of Louisville]. ProQuest Dissertations and Theses Global.

Dickie, L., Surgenor, L. J., Wilson, M., & McDowall, J. (2012). The structure and reliability of the Clinical Perfectionism Questionnaire. *Personality and Individual Differences, 52*(8), 865–869. https://doi.org/10.1016/j.paid.2012.02.003

Dimaggio, G., & Attinà, G. (2012). Metacognitive interpersonal therapy for narcissistic personality disorder and associated perfectionism. *Journal of Clinical Psychology, 68*(8), 922–934. https://doi.org/10.1002/jclp.21896

Dimaggio, G., MacBeth, A., Popolo, R., Salvatore, G., Perrini, F., Raouna, A., Osam, C. S., Buonocore, L., Bandiera, A., & Montano, A. (2018). The problem of overcontrol: Perfectionism, emotional inhibition, and personality disorders. *Comprehensive Psychiatry, 83*, 71–78. https://doi.org/10.1016/j.comppsych.2018.03.005

DiPrima, A. J., Ashby, J. S., Gnilka, P. B., & Noble, C. L. (2011). Family relationships and perfectionism in middle-school students. *Psychology in the Schools, 48*(8), 815–827. https://doi.org/10.1002/pits.20594

Dixon, F. A., Lapsley, D. K., & Hanchon, T. A. (2004). An empirical typology of perfectionism in gifted adolescents. *Gifted Child Quarterly, 48*(2), 95–106. https://doi.org/10.1177/001698620404800203

Downey, C. A., & Chang, E. C. (2007). Perfectionism and symptoms of eating disturbances in female college students: Considering the role of negative affect and body dissatisfaction. *Eating Behaviors, 8*(4), 497–503. https://doi.org/10.1016/j.eatbeh.2007.02.002

Dunkley, D. M., Berg, J.-L., & Zuroff, D. C. (2012). The role of perfectionism in daily self-esteem, attachment, and negative affect. *Journal of Personality, 80*(3), 633–663. https://doi.org/10.1111/j.1467-6494.2011.00741.x

Dunkley, D. M., Blankstein, K. R., & Berg, J. (2012). Perfectionism dimensions and the Five-factor Model of Personality. *European Journal of Personality, 26*(3), 233–244. https://doi.org/10.1002/per.829

Egan, S. J., Piek, J. P., Dyck, M. J., Rees, C. S., & Hagger, M. S. (2012). A clinical investigation of motivation to change standards and cognitions about failure in perfectionism. *Behavioural and Cognitive Psychotherapy, 41*(5), 565–578. https://doi.org/10.1017/s135246581200063x

Elderton, L. (2020, May 27). Faith Ringgold powerfully resists injustice with optimism. *Elephant.* https://elephant.art/faith-ringgold-painting-interview-race-gender-27052020

Esposito, R. M., Stoeber, J., Damian, L. E., Alessandri, G., & Lombardo, C. (2019). Eating disorder symptoms and the 2× 2 model of perfectionism: Mixed perfectionism is the most maladaptive combination. *Eating and Weight Disorders–Studies on Anorexia, Bulimia and Obesity, 24*(4), 749–755.

Flaxman, P. E., Ménard, J., Bond, F. W., & Kinman, G. (2012). Academics' experiences of a respite from work: Effects of self-critical perfectionism and perseverative cognition on postrespite well-being. *Journal of Applied Psychology, 97*(4), 854–865. https://doi.org/10.1037/a0028055

Flett, G. L., Coulter, L.-M., Hewitt, P. L., & Nepon, T. (2011). Perfectionism, rumination, worry, and depressive symptoms in early adolescents. *Canadian Journal of School Psychology, 26*(3), 159–176. https://doi.org/10.1177/0829573511422039

Flett, G. L., Hewitt, P. L., Besser, A., Su, C., Vaillancourt, T., Doucher, D., Munro, Y., Davidson, L. A., & Gale, O. (2016). The child-adolescent perfectionism scale: Development, psychometric properties, and associations with stress, distress, and psychiatric symptoms. *Journal of Psychoeducational Assessment, 34*(7), 634-652. https://doi.org/10.1177/0734282916651381

Flett, G. L., Hewitt, P. L., Blankstein, K. R., & Pickering, D. (1998). Perfectionism in relation to attributions for success or failure. *Current Psychology, 17,* 249–262. https://doi.org/10.1007/s12144-998-1010-y

Frasier, M. M., & McCannon, C. (1981). Using bibliotherapy with gifted children. *Gifted Child Quarterly, 25*(2), 81–85. https://doi.org/10.1177/001698628102500207

Frost, R. O., Lahart, C. M., & Rosnblate, R. (1991). The development of perfectionism: A study of daughters and their parents. *Cognitive Therapy and Research, 15,* 469–489. https://doi.org/10.1007/BF01175730

Frost, R. O., & Marten, P. A. (1990). Perfectionism and evaluative threat. *Cognitive Therapy and Research, 14,* 559–572. https://doi.org/10.1007/BF01173364

Gaudreau, P. (2012). A methodological note on the interactive and main effects of dualistic personality dimensions: An example using the 2 x 2 model of perfectionism. *Personality and Individual Differences, 52*(1), 26–31. https://doi.org/10.1016/j.paid.2011.08.022

Gautreau, C. M., Sherry, S. B., Mushquash, A. R., & Stewart, S. H. (2015). Is self-critical perfectionism an antecedent of or a consequence of social anxiety, or both? A 12-month, three-wave longitudinal study. *Personality and Individual Differences, 82,* 125–130. https://doi.org/10.1016/j.paid.2015.03.005

Gnilka, P. B., Ashby, J. S., & Noble, C. M. (2013). Adaptive and maladaptive perfectionism as mediators of adult attachment styles and depression, hopelessness, and life satisfaction. *Journal of Counseling & Development, 91*(1), 78–86. https://doi.org/10.1002/j.1556-6676.2013.00074.x

Gong, X., Fletcher, K. L., & Bolin, J. H. (2015). Dimensions of perfectionism mediate the relationship between parenting styles and coping. *Journal of Counseling & Development, 93*(3), 259–268. https://doi.org/10.1002/jcad.12024

Hamachek, D. E. (1978). Psychodynamics of normal and neurotic perfectionism. *Psychology: A Journal of Human Behavior, 15*(1), 27–33.

Handley, A. K., Egan, S. J., Kaney, R. T., & Rees, C. S. (2014). The relationships between perfectionism, pathological worry and generalised anxiety disorder. *BMC Psychiatry, 14,* Article 98. https://doi.org/10.1186/1471-244X-14-98

Harris, P. W., Pepper, C. M., & Maack, D. J. (2008). The relationship between maladaptive perfectionism and depressive symptoms: The mediating role of rumination. *Personality and Individual Differences, 44*(1), 150–160. https://doi.org/10.1016/j.paid.2007.07.011

He, X. (2016). When perfectionism leads to imperfect consumer choices: The role of dichotomous thinking. *Journal of Consumer Psychology, 26*(1), 98–104. https://doi.org/10.1016/j.jcps.2015.04.002

Hébert, T. P. (1991). Meeting the affective needs of bright boys through bibliotherapy. *Roeper Review, 13*(4), 207–212. https://doi.org/10.1080/02783199109553360

Hébert, T. P. (2009). Guiding gifted teenagers to self-understanding through biography. In J. L. VanTassel-Baska, T. L. Cross, & F. R. Olenchak (Eds.), *Social-emotional curriculum with gifted and talented students* (pp. 259–288). Prufrock Press.

Hébert, T. P. (2020). *Understanding the social and emotional lives of gifted students* (2nd ed.). Prufrock Press.

Hewitt, P. L., Caelian, C. F., Chen, C., & Flett, G. L. (2014). Perfectionism, stress, daily hassles, hopelessness, and suicide potential in depressed psychiatric adolescents. *Journal of Psychopathology and Behavioral Assessment, 36*(4), 663–674. https://doi.org/10.1007/s10862-014-9427-0

Hewitt, P. L., Caelian, C. F., Flett, G. L., Sherry, S. B., Collins, L., & Flynn, C. A. (2002). Perfectionism in children: Associations with depression, anxiety, and anger. *Personality and Individual Differences, 32*(6), 1049–1061. https://doi.org/10.1016/S0191-8869(01)00109-X

Hewitt, P. L., Newton, J., Flett, G. L., & Callander, L. (1997). Perfectionism and suicide ideation in adolescent psychiatric patients. *Journal of Abnormal Child Psychology, 25*(2), 95–101. https://doi.org/10.1023/a:1025723327188

Hill, A. P., Hall, H. K., & Appleton, P. R. (2012). An assessment of the similarities between a measure of positive perfectionism and a measure of conscientious achievement striving. *Psychology of Sport and Exercise, 13*(3), 353–359. https://doi.org/10.1016/j.psychsport.2011.09.003

Huprich, S. K., Porcerelli, J., Keaschuk, R., Binienda, J., & Engle, B. (2008). Depressive personality disorder, dysthymia, and their relationship to perfectionism. *Depression and Anxiety, 25*(3), 207–217. https://doi.org/10.1002/da.20290

Inglés, C. J., García-Fernández, J. M., Vicent, M., Gonzálvez, C., & Sanmartín, R. (2016). Profiles of perfectionism and school anxiety: A review of the 2 x 2 model of dispositional perfectionism in child population. *Frontiers in Psychology, 7.* https://doi.org/10.3389/fpsyg.2016.01403

IPL. (1996). *Author page: Avi.* https://www.ipl.org/div/askauthor/Avi.html

Kenney-Benson, G. A., & Pomerantz, E. M. (2005). The role of mothers' use of control in children's perfectionism: Implications for the devel-

opment of children's depressive symptoms. *Journal of Personality,*
73(1), 23–46. https://doi.org/10.1111/j.1467-6494.2004.00303.x

Kline, B. E., & Short, E. B. (1991). Changes in emotional resilience: Gifted
adolescent females. *Roeper Review, 13*(3), 118–121. https://doi.org/10
.1080/02783199109553333

Kowal, A., & Pritchard, D. (1990). Psychological characteristics of children who suffer from headache: A research note. *Journal of Child*
Psychology and Psychiatry, 31(4), 637–649. https://doi.org/10.1111/j.
1469-7610.1990.tb00803.x

Laurenti, H. J., Bruch, M. A., & Haase, R. F. (2008). Social anxiety and
socially prescribed perfectionism: Unique and interactive relationships
with maladaptive appraisal of interpersonal situations. *Personality*
and Individual Differences, 45(1), 55–61. https://doi.org/10.1016/j.
paid.2008.02.018

Limburg, K., Watson, H. J., Hagger, M. S., & Egan, S. J. (2017). The relationship between perfectionism and psychopathology: A meta-analysis.
Journal of Clinical Psychology, 73(10), 1301–1326. https://doi.org/10.
1002/jclp.22435

Maksic, S., & Iwasaki, K. (2009). Perfectionism of academically gifted primary school students: The case of Japan. *Gifted & Talented Interna-*
tional, 24(2), 51–60.

McArdle, S., & Duda, J. L. (2004). Exploring social-contextual correlates
of perfectionism in adolescents: A multivariate perspective. *Cognitive*
Therapy and Research, 28, 765–788. https://doi.org/10.1007/s10608-
004-0665-4

Miller, A. L., Lambert, A. D., & Speirs Neumeister, K. L. (2012). Parenting
style, perfectionism, and creativity in high-ability and high-achieving
young adults. *Journal for the Education of the Gifted, 35*(4), 344–365.
https://doi.org/10.1177/0162353212459257

Mofield, E. L., & Chakraborti-Ghosh, S. (2010). Addressing multidimensional perfectionism in gifted adolescents with affective curriculum.
Journal for the Education of the Gifted, 33(4), 479–513. https://doi.
org/10.1177/016235321003300403

Morelock, M. J. (1992). Giftedness: The view from within. *Understanding*
Our Gifted, 4(3), 1, 11–15.

O'Brien, D. R. (2005). *Distinguishing between students with and without*
learning disabilities: A comparative analysis of cognition, achievement,
perceptual skills, behavior, and executive functioning (Publication

No. 3209081) [Doctoral dissertation, Widener University]. ProQuest Dissertations and Theses Global.

O'Connor, R. C. (2007). The relations between perfectionism and suicidality: A systematic review. *Suicide and Life-Threatening Behavior, 37*(6), 698–714. https://doi.org/10.1521/suli.2007.37.6.698

Ogurlu, U. (2020). Are gifted students perfectionistic? A meta-analysis. *Journal for the Education of the Gifted, 43*(3), 227–251. https://doi.org/10.1177/0162353220933006

O'Leary, N., & Schuler, P. A. (2003, November). *Perfectionism in parents of gifted students* [Paper presentation]. Annual Conference of the National Association for Gifted Children, Indianapolis, IN, United States.

Öngen, D. E. (2009). The relationships between perfectionism and aggression among adolescents. *Procedia–Social and Behavioral Sciences, 1*(1), 1073–1077. https://doi.org/10.1016/j.sbspro.2009.01.193

Parker, W. D., Portesová, S., & Stumpf, H. (2001). Perfectionism in mathematically gifted and typical Czech students. *Journal for the Education of the Gifted, 25*(2), 138–152. https://doi.org/10.1177/016235320102500203

Parker, W. D., & Stumpf, H. (1995). An examination of the Multidimensional Perfectionism Scale with a sample of academically talented children. *Journal of Psychoeducational Assessment, 13*(4), 372–383. https://doi.org/10.1177/073428299501300404

Pritchard, M. E., Wilson, G. S., & Yamnitz, B. (2007). What predicts adjustment among college students? A longitudinal panel study. *Journal of American College Health, 56*(1), 15–21. https://doi.org/10.3200/JACH.56.1.15-22

Radhu, N., Daskalakis, Z. J., Arpin-Cribbie, C. A., Irvine, J., & Ritvo, P. (2012). Evaluating a web-based cognitive-behavioral therapy for maladaptive perfectionism in university students. *Journal of American College Health, 60*(5), 357–366. https://doi.org/10.1080/07448481.2011.630703

Renzulli, J. S. (1986). The three-ring conception of giftedness: A developmental model for creative productivity. In R. J. Sternberg & J. Davidson (Eds.), *Conceptions of giftedness* (pp. 53–92). Cambridge University Press.

Rhuday-Perkovich, O. (2020). *11 inspiring illustrated biographies that introduce children to diverse heroes.* https://www.readbrightly.com/illustrated-biographies-that-introduce-kids-to-diverse-heroes

Rice, K. G., Ashby, J. S., & Slaney, R. B. (2007). Perfectionism and the five-factor model of personality. *Assessment, 14*(4), 385–398. https://doi.org/10.1177/1073191107303217

Rice, K. G., Tucker, C. M., & Desmond, F. F. (2008). Perfectionism and depression among low-income chronically ill African American and White adolescents and their maternal parent. *Journal of Clinical Psychology in Medical Settings, 15*(3), 171–181. https://doi.org/10.1007/s10880-008-9119-6

Rozental, A., Shafran, R., Wade, T., Egan, S., Nordgren, L. B., Carlbring, P., Landström, A., Roos, S., Skoglund, M., Thelander, E., Trosell, L., Örtenholm, A., & Andersson, G. (2017). A randomized controlled trial of internet-based cognitive behavior therapy for perfectionism including an investigation of outcome predictors. *Behaviour Research and Therapy, 95*, 79–86. https://doi.org/10.1016/j.brat.2017.05.015

Saddler, C. D., & Buckland, R. L. (1995). The Multidimensional Perfectionism Scale: Correlations with depression in college students with learning disabilities. *Psychological Reports, 77*(2), 483–490. https://doi.org/10.2466/pr0.1995.77.2.483

Sato, S. (2020). *Sumi-e: All you need to know about Japanese ink painting.* Japan Objects. https://japanobjects.com/features/sumie

Siegle, D., & Schuler, P. A. (2000). Perfectionism differences in gifted middle school students. *Roeper Review, 23*(1), 39–44. https://doi.org/10.1080/02783190009554060

Silverman, L. K. (1993a). A developmental model for counseling the gifted. In L. K. Silverman (Ed.), *Counseling the gifted and talented* (pp. 51–78). Love.

Silverman, L. K. (1993b). The gifted individual. In L. K. Silverman (Ed.), *Counseling the gifted and talented* (pp. 3–28). Love

Sondergeld, T. A., Schultz, R. A., & Glover, L. K. (2007). The need for research replication: An example from studies on perfectionism and early gifted adolescents. *Roeper Review, 29*(5), 19–25. https://doi.org/10.1080/02783193.2007.11869220

Speirs Neumeister, K. L. (2004). Understanding the relationship between perfectionism and achievement motivation in gifted college students. *Gifted Child Quarterly, 48*(3), 219–231. https://doi.org/10.1177/001698620404800306

Stoeber, J. (2012). The 2 × 2 model of perfectionism: A critical comment and some suggestions. *Personality and Individual Differences, 53*(5), 541–545. https://doi.org/10.1016/j.paid.2012.04.029

Stoeber, J., & Stoeber, F. S. (2009). Domains of perfectionism: Prevalence and relationships with perfectionism, gender, age, and satisfaction with life. *Personality and Individual Differences, 46*(4), 530–535. https://doi.org/10.1016/j.paid.2008.12.006

Suddarth, B. H., & Slaney, R. B. (2001). An investigation of the dimensions of perfectionism in college students. *Measurement and Evaluation in Counseling and Development, 34*(3), 157–165. https://doi.org/10.1080 /07481756.2002.12069032

Tannenbaum, A. J. (1992). Early signs of giftedness: Research and commentary. *Journal for the Education of the Gifted, 13,* 22–36. https:// doi.org/10.1177/016235329201500202

Vallance, J. K. H., Dunn, J. G. H., & Dunn, J. L. C. (2006). Perfectionism, anger, and situation criticality in competitive youth ice hockey. *Journal of Sport and Exercise Psychology, 28*(3), 383–406. https://doi. org/10.1123/jsep.28.3.383

Vandiver, B. J., & Worrell, F. C. (2002). The reliability and validity of scores on the Almost Perfect Scale—Revised with academically talented middle school students. *Journal of Secondary Gifted Education, 13*(3), 108–119. https://doi.org/10.4219/jsge-2002-372

Waller, G., Wood, A., Miller, J., & Slade, P. (1992). The development of neurotic perfectionism: A risk factor for unhealthy eating attitudes. *British Review of Bulimia & Anorexia Nervosa, 6*(2), 57–62.

Wilson, H. E., & Adelson, J. L. (2008, Winter). Art across the curriculum: Language arts. *Teaching for High Potential, 3.*

Wimberley, T. E., Mintz, L. B., & Suh, H. (2016). Perfectionism and mindfulness: Effectiveness of a bibliotherapy intervention. *Mindfulness, 7*(2), 433–444. https://doi.org/10.1007/s12671-015-0460-1

About the Authors

Jill L. Adelson, Ph.D., has worked with children in a variety of settings, including academics, extracurriculars, and athletics, and as a parent. She taught fourth-grade self-contained gifted and talented in Newport News, VA, and some of her coaching activities included Odyssey of the Mind, softball, and the academic team. While teaching, Jill earned her master's degree in curriculum and instruction, specializing in gifted education, from William & Mary. As a teacher and graduate student, she conducted case studies on perfectionism in her own classroom. Jill left Virginia to pursue her doctorate in educational psychology with a joint specialization in gifted education and measurement, evaluation, and assessment at the University of Connecticut. Jill spent 9 years at the University of Louisville as a professor in educational psychology, measurement, and evaluation and 2 years as a research scientist at Duke University for the Talent Identification Program (Duke TIP). Jill currently is the coeditor of *Gifted Child Quarterly* and a gifted education and research consultant at Adelson Research & Consulting, LLC. She is the mother of three children, Caleb, Zoe, and Emma. As someone who has perfectionistic tendencies and behaviors, Jill understands the struggles of unhealthy perfectionism as well as the benefits of motivation and high, realistic goals in her academic pursuits, in her athletic pursuits, and as a mother.

Hope E. Wilson, Ph.D., wrote this book from the perspective of both a parent and an educator. As an educator, she has worked primarily as an elementary art teacher in Texas. In this position, she had the joy of teaching all students from kindergarten through fifth grade and working with the other teachers to develop cross-curricular activities and connections. Hope earned her master's degree in teaching from Austin College in Sherman, TX, and then a second master's degree in gifted education from Hardin-Simmons University in Abilene, TX. After 4 years of teaching, Hope went to the University of Connecticut to pursue her Ph.D. in educational psychology with a specialization in gifted education. For 3 years, Hope was a professor at Stephen F. Austin State University. Currently, she is an associate professor and faculty assessment coordinator at the University of North Florida and an associate editor for the *Journal of Advanced Academics*. She is the mother of two children, Lily and Keenan. A lifelong perfectionist herself, having children made Hope really consider priorities and refocus her life in order to change unhealthy perfectionism into healthy motivation.